SOCIAL INSECURITY

SOCIAL
INSECURITY

401(k)s and the Retirement Crisis

JAMES W. RUSSELL

Beacon Press
Boston

BEACON PRESS
Boston, Massachusetts
www.beacon.org

Beacon Press books
are published under the auspices of
the Unitarian Universalist Association of Congregations.

17 16 15 14   8 7 6 5 4 3 2 1

This book is printed on acid-free paper that meets the uncoated paper
ANSI/NISO specifications for permanence as revised in 1992.

Text design and composition by Kim Arney

Library of Congress Cataloging-in-Publication Data

Russell, James W., 1944-
Social insecurity : 401(k)s and the retirement crisis / James W. Russell.
      pages   cm
Includes bibliographical references and index.
ISBN 978-0-8070-1256-7 (hardcover : alk. paper)
ISBN 978-0-8070-1257-4 (ebook)
1. 401(k) plans—United States. 2. Pensions—United States.
3. Social security—United States. I. Title.
HD7105.45.U6R87 2013
332.024'01450973—dc23
2013043335

*For the activists working for pension rights
and to defend Social Security*

Contents

Preface

On my sixty-fifth birthday, instead of looking forward to retirement, I found myself addressing an overflow crowd of a hundred forty people at a university. I had, with a number of other people, organized a group called the Connecticut Committee for Equity in Retirement. We were speaking at forums for state employees throughout the state about the crisis in our 401(k)-like retirement plan. The crisis was that there would not be enough money for any of us to retire without taking severe plunges in our standards of living. We knew that because the previous spring our employer, the State of Connecticut, was having severe budgetary problems and had offered an incentive for high-seniority employees at the top of their pay scales (such as me) to retire. The state assumed it could save money if we retired. We would be replaced by new, lower-salary employees—or not replaced at all.

I say that we were in a 401(k)-*like* plan because technically we were in a 401(a) plan. Both are named after provisions of the Internal Revenue Service code that deal with a common approach to retirement: build up individual stock market investment accounts to finance retirement income. This approach differs radically from that of traditional pensions and Social Security, as we will see. The only difference between a 401(k) plan and the 401(a) we had is that our employer was in the public rather than private sector. There are a number of other 401(k)-like employer-sponsored plans such as 403(b)s and 457s. The

401(k) plans are simply more recognized because more people have them. Individual Retirement Accounts, though not employer sponsored, follow the same approach of attempting to build up income for retirement through stock market investing.

State employees in Connecticut, as well as most other states, are divided between a minority group (mostly working for state colleges and universities) who have the 401(k)-like plans and the majority who still have traditional pensions. The state's early retirement plan turned out to be a test between the two different approaches. One could logically assume that if the retirement approaches were equally beneficial, there would be roughly equal proportions of employees from the two different plans who would accept the early retirement offer.

The results, though, were astounding. More than 40 percent of eligible state employees in the traditional pension accepted the offer, versus only 1 percent in the 401(a) plan. Part of the reason, but only a small part, was that more members of the traditional pension plan accepted the early retirement offer because it was very generous to them. It gave them three extra years of credit, which would mean approximately 5 percent to 6 percent more income for the rest of their lives, amounting in some cases to over $100,000. Members of the other plan were offered a payment of only $6,000 to be spread over three years— what we bitterly referred to as a tinfoil handshake. By far the largest reason, though, why members of our 401(a) plan did not accept the early retirement offer was because we could not afford to retire based on the inadequate values of our stock market portfolios.

So here I stood in front of a hundred forty faculty members and administrators at the University of Connecticut on my sixty-fifth birthday. According to my retirement plan, sixty-five is the usual retirement age. But I had nowhere near the amount of money that I would need to continue to live in retirement more or less the way I live now. The experts tell us that we should have between 70 percent and 100 percent of our final salaries as income during retirement. By my calculation, I had somewhere around 45 percent to 50 percent by combining my 401(a) plan and Social Security projected incomes.

Some might think that it had been my fault as well as the faults of all the others who came up or would come up short at retirement time. Maybe I didn't save enough money. We are constantly urged to put away more money from our take-home paychecks. I am writing these lines, in fact, during National Save for Retirement Week, an occasion promoted by the financial services industry.

I believe in saving. I have had a savings account ever since I had a paper route in Muskogee, Oklahoma, which was my first real job when I was twelve years old. Immediately, I set up a savings account. I don't think there's ever been a time since then that I've not held some savings, however small. Even in the worst of times when I've been unemployed, I've still managed to keep some savings as a reserve. That just happens to be the way I live my life. In a certain way, this message to save for retirement resonated with me and I did put away money. For a number of years after I paid off my house, I put a sum equivalent to the former mortgage payment into my retirement account. That was in addition to what was normally deducted from my paycheck.

Most people I know did not do this. I am not pointing a finger at them, nor am I trying to win a merit badge for my savings habit. I understand why they did not do this. I did it because I have always tried to live a frugal life and believe in the virtue of saving. Many people think I am a cheapskate as a result. At the same time, I understand that it's very difficult for people to save beyond normal savings for retirement, especially if they are still making house mortgage payments. Until the Great Recession in 2008, the price of houses was only going up. People were paying higher and higher percentages of their incomes for their homes.

People with children have considerable additional expenses. When children become college age, college must be paid for. College education has become increasingly expensive. I say that as someone who has made a living from teaching in college. When I began teaching, the cost of public higher education was very affordable, but no longer is. For the 2012–2013 academic year, average tuition and fees at public four-year colleges and universities were 3.57 times what they were for the 1982–1983 year.[1] For the same period, average per capital income was only 1.37 times higher.[2]

All this together—how much you have to pay for a house, how much you have to pay for college, how much you have to pay for normal living expenses—makes it very difficult to save money for retirement. Despite all those odds, I was able to save some money. So my inability to retire cannot be blamed on the lack of a savings ethic.

Maybe I did not invest wisely. I'm not an expert investor, nor do I want to be. I do not wish to spend my days worrying about whether my investments are going up or down. There are other things I want to do with my time. Some people enjoy following the stock market and find that interesting and exciting. They can live their lives that way. Most people, though, are probably more like me and have neither the knowledge nor the interest to become expert investors.

Nevertheless, I did not invest in a totally foolish way. I diversified my investments. As a result, when the stock market crashed in 2008, I lost about 25 percent of what I had accumulated.

Those of us who have 401(k)-type retirement accounts live the myth of Sisyphus: just when we think we're really doing well, just when we think that our money is building up at a very nice rate, it falls back down again and we have to begin not exactly over again. But we have to build it up again. You might console yourself by thinking that eventually it will come back. There's no reason to worry every time the money falls back. But—and this is an important problem—rebuilding takes added time that means it will take that much longer to achieve enough money to be able to retire.

The real question is whether anyone with ordinary incomes and working lives can ever acquire enough money to retire adequately with these accounts. After a lot of study, I and many others have concluded that the answer is no despite what a financial services industry that profits handsomely from this approach to retirement financing is constantly telling us.

But, if you had told me several years ago that on my sixty-fifth birthday I would be standing in front of a crowd trying to urge people to do something about our common retirement problem, I would've thought that was crazy. Not, however, because I didn't have a history of being in front of a crowd trying to urge them to do something. I have a past that goes back to the civil rights movement in Oklahoma. I took part in lunch-counter sit-ins. I organized a protest that led to the desegregation of a school system. Since the 1960s, I have believed that when people see injustices, they should not just adapt to them or accept them. They should try to overcome them, and not just for themselves, but as part of a common struggle with people who have the same problem. We are in bad situations together and get out of them together.

I first looked at my retirement prospects in the mid-1990s when the stock market was growing very rapidly. I was not convinced that the bull market would last forever. What goes up must come down. When I calculated the benefit differences between my 401(a) plan and the traditional pension plan that other state workers had, I realized that the problem was far deeper than the unpredictability of stock market investments. I was shocked to find out that even with a bull market, I would receive less than half of what people in the pension plan would receive, and my employee contributions were more than double theirs.

I began to discuss this revelation with coworkers. But either most didn't believe me or the subject was so complicated that they didn't want to put energy into trying to understand it. Their eyes would glaze over. They'd glance at their watches. Also, because what I was saying was so contrary to what they had been led to believe, many probably thought I had gone wacko.

Their reactions were not unusual. They reflected a larger trend in which people do not take an interest in retirement and don't know much about it. They don't pay attention, partly because for most retirement is a long way off. People do not retire every day. When they start working, they are like young people who think they are immortal. The idea of retirement is remote. When these employees look at their incomes, they think only of take-home pay, not retirement.

Retirement is also a very complicated subject. Its financing is complicated. There are different approaches to it, and within those different approaches, there are more variations. Quite often, especially in the case of 401(k)s, the companies present particularly complicated information. In my own plan, we receive a large document filled with financial information. The problem is that most people don't understand what that information is. Economics researcher Robert Hiltonsmith set out to uncover the fees that he was paying for his 401(k) plan. Instead, he found that they were hidden, embedded within other figures on his statement.[3] Most have no understanding of their 401(k) statements beyond whether the balances are going up or down. Because the information is so complicated, many people simply don't want to think about it. Combining the incomprehensibility of the information with the fact that retirement is not an immediate problem produces a recipe for avoidance. Workers only begin to pay attention when they are about to retire and find that what they had assumed was not the case, that their future will be one in which they have far less income than they had thought.

Many people believe that they have much more money than they do because they see the size of the 401(k) or similar plans continuing to grow in normal market times. They have more money in them than they have in their checking accounts or in their savings accounts, if they have savings accounts. They assume that they must have a lot of money. The problem is that there's a difference between the amount of the money in the account and how far it will go in retirement.

Most people who have 401(k)s do not really understand what will happen when they actually retire. Their attention is fixed on the accumulation of funds that go up and up, except when stock market dips and crashes send them down. But once they retire, money no longer goes into the 401(k), but has to come out in order to support retirement. Most people have not thought about that and do not understand how that money is used in retirement or the various options involved in using it.

Many are averse to planning the future and live in the present. The future—in this case, retirement—is something so abstract that people simply do not pay attention to it. People who do think about retirement tend to trust experts and financial consultants. Financial consultancy is an occupation that has grown with the advent of retirement plans in which individuals must bear all the risk of investing. Most financial consultants have a monetary interest in getting people involved in particular retirement plans. They might present the information in such a way as to steer people into products that they sell.

All these reasons make it that much easier for the financial services industry to swindle employees. It is the perfect swindle because retirement income can be robbed, stolen, diverted, or taken without affecting take-home income. Because of that, people don't realize that their future money is being systematically taken from them.

In this case, the swindler is a Wall Street–aligned financial services industry that has expanded enormously with the shift to 401(k)-like market accounts. Since 1970, it has tripled its share of gross domestic product and the proportion of all corporate profits from 19.1 percent to 27.1 percent.[4] Administration fees and commissions from managing retirement savings have swelled its revenue and profits. CEO bonuses are the most outrageous tip of the iceberg.

By the time I was addressing that crowd at a university, it was clear that the only solution to our problem would be a reform allowing us to transfer from what we judged to be a failing 401(a) retirement plan to the state's traditional pension plan, which would enable us to retire without taking a plunge in our standard of living.

What we were experiencing was a microcosm of what the whole country had been experiencing since the 1980s, when 401(k) and similar plans began to significantly replace traditional pensions. In 1981, 59 percent of private-sector employees who had retirement plans had traditional defined benefit pension plans. That shrank dramatically to 19 percent in 2010, with 81 percent now having 401(k)-like plans.[5] According to a recent study of 2.2 million large-company employees who had these types of plans, 85 percent will not "have sufficient resources to meet their needs if they retire at age 65."[6] It was also a microcosm of international shifts going back to 1981, when a Chilean military dictatorship replaced the country's traditional national pension system with a stock market investment scheme similar to the one in Connecticut.

The 2008 stock market crash shook my coworkers out of their retirement complacency and prompted the formation of our organization. It also shook people throughout the country with similarly deficient retirement funds, producing a number of parallel organizing attempts to resolve the growing retirement crisis. And there have been reform efforts in other countries, including Chile, that have been victims of the same retirement swindle.

MANUFACTURED MYTHS

Pure self-interest forced me to learn everything I could about retirement plans: their design, financing, and benefits. The more I learned, the more I realized that conservative think tanks and the financial services industry had engaged in a disingenuous campaign to convince the public that 401(k)s were the best—indeed, the *only*—viable approach to retirement. This campaign manufactured the following myths for public consumption:

- The 401(k) plans produce higher rates of return than traditional pensions or Social Security.
- The 401(k) plans are cheaper for employers and employees than traditional pensions.
- Social Security is going broke and therefore needs to be privatized or reduce its benefits.
- Unfunded liabilities of overly generous public employee pensions will require taxpayer bailouts.
- There is no fiscally sustainable alternative to 401(k)s.
- Only when individuals do not save enough do 401(k)s fail to provide adequate retirement income.

None are true. Traditional pensions and Social Security produce higher returns at lower cost than 401(k)s. In fact, Social Security—the backbone of retirement security in this country—is the federal government's most successful and popular program. It provides an alternative lower-cost public-option retirement plan that performs better than private plans. For thirty years, to undermine public support for the program, conservative think tanks have disseminated false information that Social Security is financially unstable and won't be there for people when they retire, all in an effort to plant doubts in the minds of the public and make them more receptive to reforms that would privatize or reduce the program. Publicity campaigns that plant alarmist stories in the media about the unfunded liabilities of some public employee pension plans are scare tactics intended to drive wedges of resentment between the beneficiaries of these programs that actually do produce retirement security and taxpayers. Their goal is to have public employee pension plans converted to 401(k)s. As we will see, unfunded liabilities do not by themselves necessarily pose any danger to the fiscal sustainability of pension systems. It is a red herring comparable to saying that the mortgage on your house is an unfunded liability. As long as payments are properly paid, pension funds deliver their benefits in the same way that houses are paid off if mortgage payments are properly paid. The media now acknowledge that boomers are facing a retirement crisis with their 401(k)s. But they argue that it is a crisis of people's own making since they foolishly failed to save enough. The problem with that morality tale is that no one with ordinary expenses can save enough in these plans to have retirement incomes that will maintain his or her preretirement standard of living. To accuse a whole generation of participants of being improvident is to blame the victims of a gigantic swindle that forced them into plans that were loaded against them. They unknowingly never had a chance, despite all the financial services industry hype that it was a trustworthy custodian guiding their portfolios toward secure retirements gilded with opportunities to travel and other luxuries as rewards for their careers of hard work.

The manufactured myths that bolstered the swindle shifted over time. In the beginning was the promise of more generous retirement incomes than those from traditional pensions. That worked for about twenty years until it became patently obvious that the incomes would in fact be significantly less. Then the argument shifted: traditional pensions were too expensive for employers and thus not sustainable.

Participants now had to provide for themselves with supplementary savings. Workers had a moral obligation to save. If they did not, they would pay for their improvidence with poverty in their senior years. The myth that continues to be repeated in the blame-the-victim narrative is that the system can work well so long as participants do their parts and save, save, save. But, as we will see, participants would have to live as paupers in order to save enough to generate the portfolios necessary in these schemes to finance comfortable retirements.

The manufactured myth campaign has been extraordinarily successful in convincing many people to accept or at least not question changes that were not in their interest. It has created a frame of reference of assumptions about retirement plans, a complicated subject to begin with, that are as commonly held as they are false. The success of the campaign is such that alternative views have nearly been extinguished from media accounts. Large parts of the public have been conditioned to accept the best option for the financial services industry as the *only* possible plan available for them.

Whatever someone's personal retirement situation is, he or she needs to see through the widely held myths. That requires starting at the beginning: how the different systems and approaches to retirement financing work. We will see that through the 1970s, there was substantial progress in achieving a three-legged stool of retirement security with Social Security, a traditional pension, and personal savings. Then the great U-turn in retirement security began in the early 1980s as shaky 401(k) do-it-yourself investment schemes progressively replaced guaranteed pensions. Employers unloaded responsibility for maintaining solvent retirement plans, including investment risks, onto their employees, often reducing or abandoning contributions as well. How and why that happened is an international tale woven with conservative ideologues, the financial services industry, military dictators, World Bank leaders, privatizations of national retirement systems, and compliant politician enablers. The result was a massive raid on the collective retirement savings of working people to swell the profits of the financial services industry—the origin of the retirement crisis.

I wrote this book not just as a criticism of what has happened, a kind of wringing of hands. I wrote it also to show that there are grounds for hope in a small but growing international movement to resist and reject these schemes. The movement counts small-scale victories in individual workplaces to replace failing 401(k) type plans with secure pensions, to teachers that have won back pension plans after having had 401(k)s imposed on them, and to countries that have reversed privatization of their national retirement systems. This book will provoke your thinking about your personal retirement situation and national reforms to reverse the damages.

CHAPTER I

Before the Swindle

I didn't know much about Social Security during my first jobs. But I knew enough to know that it had been very helpful in my own family. My mother had worked a series of short-term jobs and only began a long-term position in her fifties as a clerical worker for the federal government. When she retired at age seventy, she had a government pension. But because she didn't have the federal position until in her fifties, the modest pension was insufficient by itself to meet her minimum retirement income needs.

Federal jobs in those years did not have Social Security coverage, but she had built up thirty-nine quarters (three-month periods of contributions) of credit from previous jobs. That was one quarter short of the forty needed to get the minimum benefit. The obvious solution was to obtain that fortieth quarter. She could get that quarter by going into business for herself and paying the Social Security taxes. She did that by turning a painting hobby into a small business and selling her paintings. She paid the Social Security tax and passed the eligibility threshold. That minimum benefit, added to her modest government pension, made all the difference.

At the time that I was helping my mother figure out her Social Security, I discovered that Social Security taxes were not being deducted from my paycheck at San Francisco State University, where I was working part-time. I called the local Social Security office. Their first response was that it was illegal. All state employees in California were supposed to be covered by Social Security. They said they would investigate. Several days later, I received a return telephone call from the office. They had found out that the State of California had a special arrangement with Social Security to exempt part-time employees such as myself from coverage. Because of that seven-year hole in my Social Security contributions, the size of my benefit would be reduced. Thank you, State of California.

What I experienced forty years ago, encapsulated by my own narrow set of problems, was the backbone of the retirement system of the United States. Forty years later, as I was approaching my own retirement, I was in a much better position to understand why it was the backbone. I was also in a better position to understand the larger picture of retirement as a societal problem.

Until relatively recently, few people had a definable period of retirement. They were born, grew up, and then worked for the rest of their lives, still toiling for their survival when they died. A thirty-year-old male in the United States in 1900 could expect, on average, to live another thirty-five years to age sixty-five, a female to sixty-six, both just on the cusp of what we today consider retirement age. As health conditions improved, people lived longer. In 2014, a thirty-year-old male can expect to live, on average, to seventy-seven, a female to eighty-one. Members of both genders can now expect to live many years in retirement.[1]

In the middle to late 1800s in some countries, increasing numbers of people began to live longer than their active involvement in work, even if the statistical average did not. As longevity increased, more people found that they could no longer work but still needed income to survive. In the 1700s and early 1800s, the great majority of people, including in the United States, lived on farms. As they became older, their work tapered off. There was a natural cycle of transitioning into retirement. Tapering off work was possible because there were other members of the farm household who could take care of people who were older.

When we think of lifespan, we have to consider a definable period of retirement and how to extend it as long as possible. When someone retires, they continue to need food, shelter, medical care, and everything else that people need to live long, healthy lives. If they have adequate food and shelter during their working lives, which declines during their retirement lives, their longevity will decrease. A key goal therefore is to ensure that when people reach retirement, their income or access to services does not sharply drop off so that they no longer have the necessary means to live. In addition, as people grow older, some of their needs increase, especially the need for medical care. Other needs may decrease, such as having enough income to support children. That's why it is necessary to consider the retirement period, in particular, to ensure that people continue to receive everything they need to live well and as long as possible.

The first kind of support from retirement occurs within households, such as when people are dependent upon younger members of their households. The driving force in farming societies was for people to have large families with more children. In a farm economy, young children could be put to work doing chores and be productive at very early ages. For adults, children were a kind of old-age insurance.

Once people left farms to live in cities—a transition that occurred massively in US history in the late 1800s and early 1900s—caring for older family members became more difficult and problematic. Families were less likely to live together in the same households. Rather than being directly produced on the land, food and other necessities for older family members had to be bought. That meant that the city family was more dependent on *money* than the farm family was.

THE THREE AGES

The farm economy was consistent with the three ages of life: before work, work, and after work. The second age group—those who are old enough to fully work—supports the first and third age groups, those too young or old to work. That has been true in all societies. Productive work provides the means for existence. We work in order to live. But not everyone can work—those too young, old, sick, or infirm. For them to survive, they must receive something from those who are able to work. Parents give from what they have to their children. They do not charge them for it.

But while the principle of the three ages has existed in every society, it has operated in different ways and conditions. In the farm economy, the first age was shorter than it is now because children became productive laborers at an earlier age. Today, people have a much longer childhood, which requires greater productivity from the second age group of working adults. People also have—and this is an interesting parallel—a much longer third age because they are living longer after leaving active work. So one condition of modern societies is that the first and third ages have lengthened and the second age group has more to support.

In the farm economy, the third age was shorter because older people, by being directly attached to a household, could continue to contribute, even to a lesser degree. An older person could have prepared meals, or if not fully in charge of meals, might have cut up vegetables or gathered fruit. They might have done some of the house cleaning or helped to watch over young children. While not as productive as people at the second age, they continued to be somewhat productive as they became older and frailer.

All of that changed as long-term economic developments undermined the viability of family farms. People moved into cities, drawn by seemingly better income opportunities in factories and other urban workplaces. It was no longer possible to maintain the close integrated organization of work and family life that farming allowed. Home was no longer the location of work. The physical separation of the two spheres of work and domestic life upset the traditional way in which the second age group could support the first and the third age groups.

For the first generation that moved off the farm and into the cities, old-age support immediately became more problematic. Many first-generation city households continued to house three generations of children, parents, and grandparents as had farm households. Grown children continued to support and live with their parents as well as their children. Grandparents provided some help in the city household as they had on the farm, but not as much. Providing for older people became more expensive because all of the goods that were self-produced on the farm had to be bought in the city economy. Also, many older people in the city did not have adult children to support them.

For the rich, old-age provision was never problematic. They had enough money to support all members of their households. They either built up more than enough money to live on during their working lives or were able to preserve inherited fortunes. The growing problem of providing for old age concerned people of ordinary and low incomes.

Parallel to the growing issue of old-age provision was a growing perceived need to provide education for the first age group—children. Family and household education was insufficient. Before the late 1800s, there were some public schools, but not enough to educate all children. In the United States, much education was private, which meant that only rich people could afford it. There was not enough public education because it was not a necessity in the farm economy. There was practical education learned through experience in how to operate a farm, but there was no need for literacy or using mathematics. To read, write, and use numbers required special training that was not considered particularly necessary in the farm economy. But as more people moved to cities, those skills became much more needed by ordinary members of the labor force.

In the 1800s, elites realized that they could not reserve education for themselves, but had to provide education for the whole society if they wanted qualified labor forces. Therefore, they looked for a way to make the whole society, rather than each individual family, responsible for educating the young. If each family bore responsibility for educating its own children, then those families that did not have the means to pay for it would be unable to educate their children. The only way to educate a whole society was if everyone took responsibility for supporting it. As a result, by the end of the 1800s, universal, free compulsory education became the norm in the United States and all other advanced societies.

There is an obvious parallel between the policy of socializing responsibility for education and socializing support for people who are no longer able to be active members of labor forces. Once again, it is the principle of the second age group taking responsibility for supporting the first and third age groups. But now it's not the second age group within a farm household taking that responsibility for its own family members who are in the first and third age groups. Society as a whole is taking responsibility for all first- and third-age members. The family ethic of the second age supporting the first and third has now became writ large in the entire society. What came together was the idea of social insurance. By pooling resources, societies could much more effectively and efficiently guard against risk than by relying solely on individual or family responsibility.

The first attempt to develop a national retirement provision system occurred in Germany in 1889. Chancellor Otto von Bismarck instituted an elementary retirement system. The initial benefits were low—about 20 percent of average pay—and did not cover all workers, but Bismarck's system established the key precedent of a government taking some responsibility for citizens' retirement.[2] In the next three and a half decades, thirty-four European nations, New Zealand, and the United States followed the German lead and developed some form of national retirement social insurance. Meanwhile, an increasing number of private employers began to offer pension coverage. Employers in the prosperous post–Civil War railroad industry offered disability and pension plans.[3] Thus, the great dividing line that ushered in modern retirement for working people was when support shifted from younger family members to governments and employers.

What evolved in the United States and in many other countries was the so-called three-legged stool of retirement planning and security. The first leg was a national retirement plan; the second, a plan sponsored by the employer; and the third, personal savings. It was never clear how long each of the legs was supposed to be. For a stool to be stable, each of the legs must be of equal length. In national retirement configurations, the legs were of different lengths. In some countries, the national system provided the bulk of retirement income. In others, employer-based plans made up the bulk. In none, though, were personal savings supposed to provide the most retirement income—an idea that would be promoted after 1980.

SOCIAL SECURITY—THE FIRST LEG

In the midst of the Great Depression, the US federal government responded to the growing need for a national retirement system with the Social Security Act of 1935. Like the European social insurance plans that preceded it, it socialized the original nineteenth-century principle of family responsibility for the elderly. Instead of each family being responsible for only its own elderly—which was an inadequate basis for supporting the entire aged population—all families would be responsible for all of the elderly. Social Security mandates that active workers and their employers pay taxes into a social security fund that supports retired workers. This formula has worked remarkably well since its inception, producing the federal government's most successful and popular domestic program.

Unlike the current contentious and partisan congressional debates on Social Security, there was no partisan divide in its inception. The Social Security Act of 1935 passed with overwhelming backing from both parties—371 to 33 in the House and 76 to 7 in the Senate. Business interests, however, including the National Association of Manufacturers, were opposed because they did not want to have to contribute employer taxes.[4]

Social Security came into being due to a confluence of factors that included need and public pressure from the grass roots. Stimulating congressional passage was the largest protest movement of the Great Depression. Dr. Francis E. Townsend, a physician and entrepreneur, mobilized hundreds of thousands into some seven thousand Townsend clubs that demanded a monthly pension of $200 for all people over sixty.[5] Unlike the bill that passed, the only criterion for eligibility was age, and beneficiaries would receive equal payments. It is doubtful that the Social Security Act would have passed without that pressure.

The Townsend movement arose during the Great Depression when the entire capitalist system was being questioned. Enough political and economic elites realized that if they didn't allow reforms like Social Security to take place, the whole system might collapse for both economic and social reasons. On the economic side, economist John Maynard Keynes argued that governments had to redistribute some income to the disadvantaged to maintain consumer demand. Social Security met that test since it would enable those too old to work to have an income with which to make consumer purchases. On the social side, unemployment and poverty, including among the elderly, could provoke rebellion if it continued to grow. Growing left-wing and right-wing leaders and organizations, from the Communist Party to Huey Long and Father Coughlin, sought radical—albeit very different—changes that would threaten the interests of traditional elites.

The major components of Social Security were retirement benefits, disability insurance, and aid to the poor. The original plan of the program was to start collecting payroll taxes in 1936 from employees and employers in commerce and industry, excluding railroads, which had their own retirement plan. That covered about 60 percent of the workforce.[6] The fund would build up before the first benefits were paid out in 1942, which was later moved up to 1940. There would be immediate benefits for the elderly poor as a transitional program until the full system kicked in.

From the beginning, Social Security collected its revenue on the basis of a flat tax—1 percent of payroll from both employers and employees—but paid out benefits progressively because it was designed to lessen elderly poverty. Lower-income workers would have higher percentages of their preretirement incomes replaced than higher-income workers would. Social Security was never designed to be a full retirement program, though it became the only retirement income that many would receive in the absence of supplementary workplace plans.

Initial benefits were, at first, very low and fixed. Once the low benefit amount was determined, it would remain the same for the rest of the retiree's life. In 1950, Congress passed major reforms to Social

Security that broadened eligibility to participate to formerly excluded categories, such as farm workers, and added a provision for a cost-of-living adjustment (COLA). In order to catch up with purchasing power lost to inflation from 1940 to 1950, the first COLA was a huge 77 percent. Other reforms expanded coverage so that, in 2009, 94 percent of the labor force was performing work covered by Social Security. The remaining major categories of noncovered work are federal employees hired before 1984, railroad workers who continue to have their own retirement system, state and government employees in noncontributory systems, and certain very low-income workers.[7]

Today, low, medium, and high earners receive, on average, 57, 42, and 35 percent, respectively, of their preretirement incomes.[8] If Social Security did not exist, an estimated 44 percent of the elderly, rather than the current 9 percent, would be poor.[9] The program also supports close to 10 million disabled persons younger than retirement age.[10]

OCCUPATIONAL PENSIONS—
THE SECOND LEG

Public-sector military and civilian employees were the first recipients of occupational pensions. In colonial times, some colonies gave disability pensions to militia members injured in Indian wars. The Continental Congress established military pensions. The first government civilian employee pensions were offered after 1850 in some cities to police and fire personnel and teachers. In 1911, Massachusetts became the first state to provide pensions for state employees. In 1920, the Federal Employees Retirement Act expanded a partial system of coverage to all federal employees.[11]

In the late 1800s, a few private employers began offering pension systems as job benefits. By the time Social Security was enacted in 1935, private pensions were more common but by no means universal—one of the reasons for the necessity of developing a national retirement system. Employers saw advantages to offering pension plans because they would reduce employee turnover and its expenses by rewarding loyalty. They also initially saw pensions as a low-cost item, since the money put aside for retirement benefits would not have to be paid out for a long time.

From the beginning, a pattern developed in which public-sector workers were more likely to be provided with pensions than private-sector workers, and public-sector pensions were more likely to have higher benefits than private-sector ones. Put differently, private-sector employers lagged and often resisted pension provision. Governments thus have covered much greater percentages of their employees and usually with better benefits than have private employers. Currently, 72 percent of public-sector workers in the United States have retirement plans, compared to just 39 percent of those in the private sector.[12] Governments, much more than private entities, have organized coverage through national retirement systems for entire populations.

Private employers and companies have been uneasy with governments taking the lead in retirement provision. Private employers in the United States have opposed their public counterparts setting high retirement benefit standards; and private insurance, investment, and other financial services companies have considered public provision of retirement benefits to be at the expense of their own potential profits.

Until 1980, most public- and private-sector retirement plans, as well as Social Security, were technically *defined benefit* plans. In those plans, participants pay into a collective pool from which benefits to retirees are paid. The pool may be a separate pension fund or part of the general revenues of a public entity. Members of defined benefit plans don't build up accounts individually. Rather, they accumulate guaranteed rights to retirement benefits.

Most defined benefit plans determine benefits according to a formula based on the number of years of participation multiplied by a percentage of the final salary. In the case of a pension plan with a multiplier of 2, a worker with twenty-five years would receive a pension amount equal to 50 percent (25 years x 2) of final salary. Actual multipliers vary from plan to plan. I have seen a range between 1 and 2.75. Members of Congress have a 2.5 multiplier, which is far above the average. The justification, according to their plan, is that it will encourage older members to retire and make way for younger ones.

Determination of what constitutes the final salary varies. In some plans, it is the grand total of income the person receives from the employer in the final year of employment. The problem with this approach is that it encourages the practice of "spiking" the final salary by artificially driving it up through overtime or other forms of dramatic salary increases, which in turn undermine the long-term financial sustainability of the fund. In reaction, a number of plans have instituted reforms, such as only considering base salaries in the calculation of benefits, requiring that the final salary figure be the average of the last three or more years, or limiting or eliminating from consideration dramatic final salary increases.

Social Security is a type of defined benefit plan, but its calculation of benefits is different from typical employer-based plans. It is based on the average of the thirty-five years of highest contributions controlled for the effects of inflation. That longer span precludes spiking. It also has progressive income redistribution built into the formula so that, as mentioned, lower-income groups achieve higher rates of income replacement than upper-income groups.

Nearly all defined benefit pensions originally operated under a strict *pay-as-you-go* principle: benefits to retirees were paid out of current revenues, which could be either general revenues for public and private entities or contributions to separate pension funds. That continues to be the system Social Security employs. The principle works so long as contributions equal or exceed benefits being paid out. Virtually all employer-based defined benefit plans supplement pay-as-you-go financing with income derived from fund balances invested in the stock market.

Any pension fund, though, is susceptible to having its fiscal balances upset if it is not properly funded. An employer might decide to skip payments in order to balance other accounts. A shrinking workforce will result in fewer employees supporting more retirees. Managers may decide to divert temporary pension surpluses to other uses, such as funding medical benefits, leaving the funds vulnerable during periods of stock market losses.[13] The more there is such funding volatility, the more likely the fund's long-term sustainability will be undermined.

The Studebaker Corporation, which manufactured automobiles, went out of business in 1963. Its pension fund had been so poorly funded that many of its workers were left with severely reduced or no retirement benefits. The Studebaker experience encouraged congressional action that resulted in the Employee Retirement Income Security Act (ERISA) of 1974. ERISA requires that private employers with defined benefit plans maintain minimum funding. ERISA also established the Pension Benefit Guarantee Corporation to insure private pension funds. In the event of a private company's bankruptcy, the Pension Benefit Guarantee Corporation acts as a backup so that retirees continue to receive at least part of their pensions.

The possibility of bankruptcy and other disruptions stimulated the call for *prefunding* of pensions. With a fully pay-as-you-go system, if contributions stop, as when a company goes out of business, pension payments have to stop too and current workers will receive nothing for their contributions. The idea of prefunding, which ERISA called for, is to build up enough of a reserve in pension funds so that, should contributions stop, there will be enough to keep paying pensions for the rest of retirees' lives and pay off current workers for what they have contributed. That is a prudent, fiscally conservative goal. Any pension fund can be measured according to how close it has come to achieving it. Some pension funds are fully funded, others overfunded, and others underfunded.

Being underfunded in itself is not a serious problem so long as enough contributions are coming in to meet current—as opposed to all current and future—obligations. Public-sector pension funds have more leeway in this respect than do private ones. ERISA funding regulations do not apply to public-sector funds, which allow them to be more underfunded than private plans. With the exception of small towns and cities, there has been no danger of public entities going bankrupt.

The balance between revenues and expenses does not need to be reformed if there is progress toward full funding. Even if progress is stalled or going in the other direction, there may be no fiscal need for reform if the condition is temporary, as when a recession decreases revenues from pension fund investments—which beleaguered many public and private pension funds after the 2008 stock market crash.

Reforms are only needed for those pension funds whose balances of unfunded liabilities are growing on a long-term basis. In the worst of those cases, slight changes in contribution rates deliver dramatic revenue increases. Such abuses as spiking can and should be eliminated. Employer underfunding by skipping contributions that are not recaptured can be reduced or eliminated. Early retirement incentive programs that offer workers unearned pension credits can be eliminated.

There are multiple ways to maintain that favorable balance between pension revenue and expenses and make progress toward full funding. They start with the two sources of fund income: contributions and earnings from investments. Contributions can, of course, increase or decrease. If they grow, through either increased employer contributions or increased employee contributions, the size of the pool will grow. They could also increase if more employees are hired—if the ratio between active workers and retired workers increases. The opposite condition is that, if employers or employees decrease contributions for whatever reason, the amount in the pool will decrease.

The ratio between active and retired workers also can be affected by increasing or decreasing the minimum retirement age. If the minimum age of retirement is changed, say from sixty-five to sixty-six, there will be more active workers in proportion to retired workers and the size of the pool from which to pay benefits will increase.

A variable feature of defined benefit plans, but one of critical importance, is whether they contain COLAs. If a retiree receives a $25,000 annual pension, unless it contains a COLA that allows the income to rise with inflation, the *real* income will decline over time. Social Security has a built-in COLA, but not all occupational pensions do.

Most defined benefit pensions are set up to include surviving spouses. In a typical pension, upon retirement, the participant has payout options. Single or widowed retirees receive pensions for the rest of their lives. Spouses can be included in pension plans, so that once the participant dies, they continue to receive payments. In a typical pension plan, surviving spouses will receive either 50 or 100 percent of the original pension payment. Each of the three payout options—single life, surviving spouse at 50 percent, and surviving spouse at 100 percent—has different individual payment amounts. Single life is the highest, and the surviving spouse at 100 percent is the lowest.

SUMMING UP

Through the 1970s, there was clear progress in developing retirement security in the United States. Each generation on average enjoyed more retirement security than the previous one. Social Security—the first leg of the stool—expanded coverage from 55 percent of the civilian workforce in 1939 to 91 percent in 1979. The size of its benefits increased substantially in 1950. Thus, while average earners retiring at age sixty-five in 1940 received only 26.2 percent of their preretirement incomes, in 1979, they were receiving 48.1 percent.[14] Almost half of workers were participating in occupational defined benefit pension plans—the second leg. These included the great majority of public employees and the majority of the minority of private employees who had retirement plans. The third leg of individual retirement savings, however, was so paltry that it was clear it could not be relied upon. The system was more like a two-wheel bicycle—with different-sized wheels—than three-legged stool.

Not all was well. Occupational pension coverage rates lagged far behind that of Social Security. Less than half of workers had such plans. Put differently, most workers had something by virtue of Social Security, but it, unlike a number of European national retirement systems, was not designed to provide the bulk of retirement income replacement. The different situations of those with and without occupational pensions produced very uneven retirement incomes and security. The critical next task was to fill in the gaps so that more workers, like those who had both Social Security and occupational pensions, would have adequate income replacement upon retirement. What happened, though, was very different.

CHAPTER 2

A Fix for
What Wasn't Broken

Milton Friedman, a University of Chicago economics professor, had the distinction of being the first and so far the only American intellectual to have a formative influence on social and public policy. Whereas European policies can be traced back to particular intellectuals such as John Maynard Keynes, Emile Durkheim, and even Karl Marx, the origins of American policies lie more in pragmatic responses to particular problems. If any names are attached to policies, they are those of politicians who were in office when the policies originated. Franklin Delano Roosevelt's name is inevitably linked to the origins of Social Security and Lyndon Baines Johnson's to Medicare.

Friedman, more than anyone else, was responsible for articulating the ideas—the ideology—that guided the 1981 conservative revolution during the Reagan administration that launched, among other changes, 401(k) plans. At the core of his ideas was a model of pure capitalism. The closer societies came to it, he maintained with near missionary zeal, the more possible it would be for them to realize the values of individual and political freedom.

Freedom is a value that no one opposes in principle. Capitalism is another matter. It has far less universal appeal. What Friedman did was to link the two by arguing that capitalism was a necessary condition for freedom. If capitalism could share the luster of the universal value of freedom, its reputation would be greatly enhanced. In the same way, others have attempted to argue that democracy, also a value with universal appeal, is inextricably linked to capitalism. Socialists have made similar attempts to take advantage of the universal appeals of freedom and democracy to justify the economic system that they advocate.

Pure capitalism implies a system built on complete individual economic freedom. Capitalist entrepreneurs are free to run their businesses as they please, while workers (unlike slaves) are free to quit jobs and seek other ones. By implication, any government interference with capitalist economic freedom—be it from partial or full-blown socialist arrangements or even liberal regulatory ones—will by definition compromise individual freedom.

Individual economic freedom makes possible, but only possible, political freedom. Friedman was careful to point out that while capitalism was a necessary condition, it was not a sufficient condition for political freedom. Fascist systems in Spain and Italy, for example, had capitalism without political freedom. Guaranteed individual rights, as in the Bill of Rights of the US Constitution, are necessary conditions also to ensure political freedom.

Friedman made these arguments the cornerstone of his most widely read book, appropriately titled *Capitalism and Freedom.* Published in 1962, the second year of the Kennedy administration, its opening pages questioned the president's famous call to service: "Ask not what your country can do for you; ask what you can do for your country." Beneath the good-sounding message, according to Friedman, lay a threat to freedom. *Country* in his mind was a code word for government. The president's formulation explicitly assumed that government *should* do a lot for citizens, while advocating that citizens had the mutual responsibility to do a lot for government. To the contrary, in Friedman's mind, the greatest threat to individual freedom lay in the growth of government interference and coercion. In order to advance and preserve individual freedom, it was necessary to reduce the size and scope of government to a necessary minimum, just enough to provide a legal and monetary framework so that free enterprises could compete with common rules of the game. Kennedy's message went in the opposite direction by building up the nexus between individuals and their governments.

In essence, Friedman's core message contained three summary elements: maximize individual freedom, promote free enterprise and free market capitalism, and eliminate government interference with individual or economic freedom. Together, these ingredients added up to a recipe for the classic liberalism—not conservatism—of the mid-nineteenth century. A century and a half ago, conservatives in England traditionally embraced strong royalist governments, while liberals affirmed individual liberty and limited government. Friedman referred to himself as a classic liberal in this respect.[1] Only at the end of the century did liberalism become more associated with advocacy of government programs and a regulated, as opposed to laissez-faire, capitalism. In large parts of Europe, liberalism and conservatism retain their original meanings, whereas in the United States, they have changed sides. Today's conservatives and liberals are yesterday's liberals and conservatives. One contemporary convention that partially resolves this terminological confusion is to refer to Friedman and other laissez-faire advocates as neoliberals to distinguish them from liberals who advocate government regulations and programs.

One of the reasons why Friedman's message could be so influential was because he was exceptionally effective at making it. *Capitalism and Freedom*, which sold over a half-million copies, was very well written. Friedman had a style that allowed him to reach readers with plain, interesting, and persuasive writing. Yet Friedman was eloquently wrong in my view because he assumed that a capitalist system would function flawlessly only if government interference was removed, like grit out of an engine. Any examination of the actual history of capitalism, though, will show that left to its own devices, it is a crisis-prone system. The United States has suffered thirteen recessions since the Great Depression in the 1930s. The severity and frequency of economic crises were greater during the nineteenth and early twentieth centuries, when government economic regulations were slight, than during the mid- to later twentieth century, when they were more developed. On the social side, poverty was much greater before the advent of government progressive taxation and poverty-reduction social programs.

Friedman's notion of individual economic freedom is also highly lopsided. Theoretically, free labor contracts are between equal partners—a free exchange of labor for wages. Supposedly, workers freely accept the terms of employment, but they have little choice without freely available employment opportunities. Classic sociologist Max Weber thus characterized the supposed free choice that workers had in labor contracts with the appropriate Latin phrase, *coactus voluit*—it is his choice, although coerced. The freedom of a worker to quit a job is no match for the freedom of capitalists to fire workers. Even in strikes, employers usually have more resources to prevail by outlasting strikers. To obtain any parity with employers, workers would have to combine into unions to increase their individual powers, a development that would then constrain the freedom of employers.

No matter what one thinks of the validity of Friedman's pure capitalism, it was an effective message that was influential not just because it was effectively made, but also because its followers were predisposed to believe it. Marxist economist Paul Sweezy, one of the founders of the independent socialist journal *Monthly Review*, was an equally effective writer, but his message was not as welcome because not as many people were predisposed to hear it. Put differently, Friedman had a message that resonated with something that had deep cultural roots. It was logical that his message arose on American rather than European soil.

In Europe, capitalism as an economic system first developed through a centuries-long struggle with medieval feudal institutions. It never completely broke free from them; instead, it settled on compromises. The preeminent cultural institution of medieval feudalism, the Roman Catholic Church that was dominant in such European countries as France, Spain, and Italy, for example, never completely accepted the capitalist value system and continued to resist complete market determination of human relations. Then, just as capitalism seemed to be making headway against feudal institutions, especially in Protestant countries such as England and the Netherlands, a strong socialist and communist challenge developed at the end of the nineteenth century that would result in splitting the continent into separate economic systems for the better part of the past century.

Capitalism in the United States, to the contrary, as classically argued by political scientist Louis Hartz, developed on an institutional tabula rasa or blank sheet.[2] There were no preexisting feudal institutions. Also, unlike in large parts of Latin America, the indigenous population was so sparse that its preexisting institutions could be easily marginalized as capitalism rolled forward. While there have been socialist and communist parties, they never had the impact on US history that they had on European history.

It was thus no accident that Friedman developed as an intellectual in an American rather than European context. His message resonated with deep, cultural, political, historical, and economic conditions, especially as sociologist Seymour Martin Lipset emphasized, an entrenched anti-statism that was suspicious of government activity.[3] Europeans, to the contrary, are more likely to see government action and programs as means to solve their common problems, indeed, to *expect* their governments to take action. The contrast between European and American attitudes is not absolute. Friedman's neoliberal message appeals to some Europeans as well; and there are countercurrents in US history that produce substantial political public support for government regulations and social programs. Public backing for New Deal programs is an example.

Friedman's message especially resonated with business interests. They stood to gain billions of dollars to the extent that those ideas became policy. Ideas can have economic consequences, an inversion of the old belief of some Marxists that the causal direction was always the opposite. While Friedman never stated his arguments in that way, business interests were quick to understand how they would benefit. That was why they paid him well to speak at their conferences. Any reduction of government price and other regulations in the name of economic freedom would benefit their profit margins. Any reduction of taxes in the name of reducing government power would keep more income in their hands. Any reduction of government income redistribution programs to support the poor in the name of restoring individual responsibility would increase their own individual incomes. If previous to Friedman business leaders had accepted, however reluctantly or begrudgingly, limits on their power in order to maintain the stability of the economic system, they now had a welcome message that those limits were unnecessary and, indeed, counterproductive.

FRIEDMAN AND SOCIAL SECURITY

What is of special relevance to us is that Friedman urged that Social Security be abolished on the grounds it created an unnecessary government program that interfered with individual freedom and the private market.[4] Because participation in Social Security was mandatory for most workers, they were being coerced into a government program. In Friedman's opinion, individuals instead should be free to join or not join private, as opposed to government, plans that would provide for their old age. Social Security contributions were kept in a government-controlled fund rather than being available for investment in the private financial market. Social Security fostered values that were inconsistent with the type of pure capitalism that he advocated. Instead of each individual working hard to accumulate savings that would ensure her or his own retirement security, Social Security relied on a collectivist program that redistributed income to those who contributed less.

In what was his most bizarre argument, Friedman maintained that even though the program provided more income replacement for lower- than higher-income participants, it was ultimately unfair to them. Lower-income people, he reasoned, did not live as long as higher-income people. They therefore contributed relatively more and collected relatively less than higher-income people.[5] A variation of that argument is employed today by opponents of Social Security when they argue that the program is unfair to African Americans for the same reason.

Friedman was taking on the most successful and publicly supported government social program, a legacy of the New Deal. He would consistently oppose Social Security from the publication of *Capitalism and Freedom* in 1962, when he first proposed abolishing it, to the last years of his life when he criticized presidents Bill Clinton's and George W. Bush's partial privatization proposals for not going far enough. Abolition of Social Security would be a giant step toward the unfettered capitalism that he advocated. For those ideas to advance beyond his classrooms, books, articles, and public speeches—which they clearly did—required organizational and political allies.

Friedman's free market message first arose in the late 1940s, one decade after Roosevelt's New Deal, which heavily relied on Keynesian regulatory and redistributive principles. It was very much a contrarian heterodox view with the economics mainstream at that time firmly embracing and refining the Keynesian approach. By the 1950s, Friedman's views were beginning to gather more followers. Little by little, what was heterodox become orthodox.

What began to take shape in the 1960s during the Kennedy and Johnson administrations, the next highpoint in American liberalism after the Roosevelt years, was a new conservative countermovement. It was composed of intellectuals such as Friedman and William F. Buckley, conservative foundations and think tanks such as the American Enterprise Institute, and politicians like Barry Goldwater, to whom Friedman was an adviser during his 1964 run for the presidency, and then California governor Ronald Reagan.

Friedman's influence was also growing internationally. In 1956, the University of Chicago economics department, with US government and private foundation support, began a program to train Chileans. By 1963, twelve of the thirteen faculty members at the Catholic University in Santiago were graduates of the program.[6] They were fervent apostles of the Friedman free market ideology at a time when the country's main political parties of the Right and Left embraced an approach to development that relied on state industry and import substitution—anathema to free market principles. One of their most eager students was the scion of a wealthy family, José Piñera. He found Friedman's comments about abolishing Social Security in *Capitalism and Freedom* especially interesting and referred to the economics department at Catholic University as "a wholly owned subsidiary of the University of Chicago."[7]

Two gigantic fissures developed in American politics in the 1960s and 1970s to upset electoral patterns and pave the way for Friedman's laissez-capitalist message to become government policy. The civil rights movement drove a wedge between northern and southern Democrats, leading to the wholesale defection of the latter to the Republican Party. Legalization of abortion, which was favored by the liberal wing of the Democratic Party, drove a substantial part of its traditional Catholic working-class base into the arms of the Republican Party.

As a result of the political fissures, Republican Ronald Reagan won the 1980 presidential race with a hard-right domestic policy agenda nurtured by the Friedman-influenced intellectuals, conservative think tanks, and politicians of the New Right. As a reflection of the new respectability of his laissez-faire approach, in 1976 Friedman was awarded a Nobel Prize in economics.

The Reagan revolution sent a shock wave that went far beyond the borders of the country. The United States is the third most-populous country in the world after China and India. It has the world's largest gross domestic product. It has the strongest military, which has bases in over two hundred countries. Any fundamental shifts in its policy orientation have inevitable international ramifications.

The growing neoliberal influence spread to important sectors of the Democratic Party as well, producing a neoliberal consensus that covered all of the Republic Party and an increasingly powerful, so-called moderate sector of the Democratic Party. In play now were retirement savings not only in employment plans but also those in Social Security, the centerpiece liberal program of the New Deal, which Friedman and his conservative followers had always opposed and which kept the largest portion of retirement savings off-limits to the private financial services industry.

ADVENT OF 401(K)S

When the Republicans came into national office in 1981, 59 percent of people who had private employer-based retirement plans had defined benefit plans.[8] Section 401(k) had been part of the Internal Revenue

Code for just over two years. In 1978, Ted Benna, a benefits consultant, convinced the Internal Revenue Service to add subsection (k) to section 401 of the code. That enabled companies to set up plans in which employees could save tax-free for retirement. Benna essentially wanted to have the provisions of IRAs, passed in 1975, expanded to workplaces. The purported original purpose of both was to supplement defined benefit pensions, to shore up the third leg of the stool. It was unclear whether 401(k)s could be the vehicle to create primary retirement plans where none existed before or for converting existing defined benefit ones. The Republican administration moved quickly to clarify the ambiguity and gave the green light for the more ambitious interpretation of what section 401(k) allowed. The new type of retirement plan took off. Instead of 401(k)s being used to supplement defined benefit plans, they would increasingly replace them. Instead of benefits being defined and guaranteed by employers, 401(k)s absolved employers of having to guarantee benefits. They were also absolved of having to guarantee contributions despite the plans using the defined contribution label in contrast to traditional defined benefit pension plans.

Making retirement provision more dependent on individual stock market investment results was consistent with Friedman's prescriptions. The 401(k) plans placed responsibility on the individual employee to save and invest wisely in order to have future retirement income. In the meantime, their retirement savings directly contributed to private capital growth. They produced an accumulation of capital that benefited the production system. If Social Security as well as defined benefit occupational pensions were converted to 401(k) private accounts, it would be all the better, according to Friedman.

The 401(k) conversion movement proceeded rapidly among private-sector employers. In 1981, 59 percent of the private-sector workers who had retirement plans had defined benefit ones, and 41 percent had defined contribution ones. By 2010, the ratio had completely reversed: only 19 percent had defined benefit plans, while 81 percent had defined contribution ones, as defined benefit plans increasingly became an endangered species in the private sector.[9]

There are three types of mainly private-sector conversions for employer-based retirement plans. In the first, the defined benefit plan is closed to new entrants but remains the same for existing members. In the second, existing members receive defined benefit pensions when they retire based on the time already served before conversion. Subsequent retirement contributions go into a defined contribution plan. In the third, most drastic plan, the defined benefit plan is completely closed to actively working employees. Their accrued credits are converted into dollar amounts that are transferred to defined contribution plans.

The first type, in which existing workers are able to keep their existing plans but new workers receive 401(k)s, meets the least resistance. Future workers who are not able to protest take a loss in retirement security. Labor unions often get pushed into this corner. They are under enormous pressure to make concessions on retirement benefits. They know that the concession is not good for new employees, but new employees are not yet members. The current generation of workers is spared the consequences of the concession. The yet to be hired workers have no representation, so it is easy to sacrifice their interests.

The same conversion trend occurred in the United Kingdom as a result of reforms instigated by Reagan's conservative ally, Prime Minister Margaret Thatcher, who was similarly influenced by the free market theories of Friedman.[10] The UK national retirement system, the basic state pension, was funded like Social Security by employer and employee contributions. Its wage replacement rate is much lower than that of Social Security. A far larger part of retirement income came from a second tier of the retirement system, where employers and employees had to either pay into a second national system—the State Earnings-Related Pension Scheme (SERPS)—or a private pension scheme with equivalent or higher benefits. All forms of retirement income combined provided among the lowest levels of wage replacement in Europe.

In 1986, the Thatcher government pushed through the Social Security Act, which had been under consideration since 1983, to privatize SERPS on a voluntary basis. With a carrot–and–stick approach, it encouraged individuals to opt out of the system and set up their own private accounts, called personal pensions. The carrot was a 2 percent tax rebate for those who left the SERPS system; the stick, a reduction in SERPS benefits. Individuals could also leave their employer-supplied pension for the individual plans.

Thatcher's reform provided a boon for the British financial services industry, which aggressively marketed the new, alternative private retirement accounts. By 1999, one-quarter of British workers had switched out of SERPS and into the new accounts.[11] Meanwhile, by 2005, most of the largest one hundred companies that had their own defined benefit plans as alternatives to SERPS had closed them to new members.[12]

As there has been a great shift away from defined benefit retirement plans for private-sector workers in the United States and United Kingdom, defined benefit plans continue to predominate in the public sectors of both countries and frustrate the proponents of private accounts.

The 401(k) industry took off because it delivered great advantages to employers. All risks were shifted to employees. Employers no longer had to worry about whether their retirement plans were adequately funded to meet their guaranteed liabilities. By definition, defined contribution plans do not have liabilities since there are no guaranteed benefits. The issue of unfunded retirement plan liabilities had grown among employers since the 1920s and 1930s when they first began offering defined benefit pensions. Financing of those programs on pay-as-you-go bases is easiest when they are first introduced because all participants are paying into them and none are yet drawing pensions from them. A company could in theory grant a pension benefit to workers and then do nothing for years to fund it until there were actual retirees to receive payments. That is an extreme case, and few if any companies are likely to be so irresponsible. But there can be lesser degrees of irresponsibility. A company can underfund a pension plan in multiple ways. It can make no payments into the fund during recessionary periods of revenue shortfalls. It could not compensate for plan revenue losses when stock market returns were down. Many private defined benefit plans in fact went bankrupt because of underfunding.

In other cases, companies had to compensate for underfunding by transferring revenues from elsewhere.

No defined benefit plan with guaranteed benefits is sustainable if it is not properly funded, which a number of companies, including the Studebaker Corporation, failed to do. Closing down those plans stopped the future growth of liabilities. The new defined contribution plans that took their places were liability-free. What was good for the accounting books, though, was at the expense of employees who lost the security of guaranteed benefits. All of the companies that had not properly funded their pension plans found attractive the idea that they could absolve themselves of retirement responsibilities with a onetime contribution to a worker's 401(k) account and then not worry about that plan's performance.

There were also overfunded defined benefit plans that had surpluses. For a number of corporations, conversions to defined contribution plans presented opportunities to appropriate these surpluses for other purposes. Once the defined benefit plan was closed, the corporation could pocket the remaining surplus. In some cases, the pocketing was simply an added benefit for the conversion; in others, it was the prime motive. In 1986, as the 401(k) conversions were accelerating, Exxon closed out its defined benefit plan and transferred its $1.6 billion surplus to its treasury.[13] A decade later, Bell Atlantic took $3 billion from its overfunded pension plan to pay the early retirement incentives for twenty-five thousand managers.[14] Raiding pension surpluses was also tempting for companies that didn't intend to close out the plan. DuPont, for example, diverted $1.7 billion from its pension surplus to pay for employee health care.[15] Robbing today's surplus, though, can cause tomorrow's unfunded liability, especially if future stock returns plunge.

CUTTING WAGES BY THE PATH OF LEAST RESISTANCE

If converting to 401(k)s gave employers a way out of responsibility for the retirement security of their workers, it also gave them a new hidden way to cut their wages. As of 2012, some 54 percent of private, state, and local employees participated in retirement plans. The contributions that their employers make to these plans are considered to be part of the employee's total compensation package. They in essence retain part of the employee's pay to fund the retirement plan under the misleading name of the employer contribution. In most cases, there are also employee contributions. Of workers in defined contribution plans, 67 percent are required to make such contributions.[16] The only difference between employer and employee contributions is that employees never see the former, while they see the latter being deducted from their paychecks. Both contributions come out of their total compensation.

With a defined benefit plan, sufficient amounts must be held back from total compensation to fund the guaranteed benefits. In such a system, the only way that employers can cut their costs is to shift the balance between the nominal employer and employee contributions and require a greater proportion from employees. Employees resist this because they see tangible reductions of their current take-home pay. The parallel is when employers attempt to have employees pay greater shares for health-care policies, often the subject of labor disputes.

If, however, employers shift to defined contribution plans, they can lower their costs, often without meeting employee resistance, because there is no reduction in current take-home pay. Because, with defined contribution plans such as 401(k)s, employers do not guarantee benefit levels, they are free to reduce contributions and therefore total compensation packages for labor. The beauty of the system, from their point of view, is that the wage reductions are largely hidden from employees and therefore often not resisted.

Recent studies in the United Kingdom have shown that contributions to defined contribution plans average only 5.8 percent of employee salaries, compared to 14.2 percent for defined benefit plans.[17] A superficial reading of that statistic would lead to the conclusion that defined contribution plans are more economical. But they are only more economical for employers. Employees are doubly harmed.

First, lower levels of contributions—that is, what the employer and employee financially invest in the plan—will fund lower levels of employee retirement incomes in either defined benefit or defined contribution systems. Second, because the contributions are going into a defined contribution system rather than defined benefit system, they will yield lower benefits. A dollar—or in this case, pound sterling—invested in a defined benefit system will always yield more than a similar amount invested in a defined contribution system (see chapter 5 for more about the multiple reasons for this). That is, a contribution to a defined benefit plan yields a much higher employee retirement benefit than an identical contribution to a defined contribution plan.

There is still another way that employers can use defined contribution plans to lower their total compensation wage costs, as my brother-in-law, who works for a newspaper, found out. During the 2008 recession when its revenues declined, the newspaper simply stopped funding his 401(k) account. I asked him if the recession was having any effect on his job. At first, he said no. His salary remained the same, and there was no danger of layoffs. Then he remembered that his employer had ceased to contribute to his 401(k) account. He didn't seem particularly worried about it. He should have been, as I tried to explain, because he was losing not only the face amount of the contribution but all that it would accumulate between then and the time of his retirement. With defined contribution plans not delivering the benefits of defined benefit plans, even in the best of times, any loss of accumulated values due to employer contribution cutbacks has serious consequences for workers. My brother-in-law's experience was not unusual. According to one study cited in the *Wall Street Journal*, 34 percent of employers either reduced or eliminated their 401(k) matches in reaction to the recession.[18]

If my brother-in-law had had a defined benefit plan instead, his employer still would have been able to withhold contributions without him particularly noticing or caring. The difference is that the employer would have suffered the consequences of the withheld payments. It would have to find a way to make up for them when my brother-in-law retired to ensure that the guaranteed pension checks could be paid. But with the 401(k), his employer was absolved of any such worry. Only my brother-in-law will suffer the consequences, which won't occur for a long time.

PORTABILITY AT A PRICE

In the 1980s, the financial services industry promoted 401(k) and other defined contribution plans as good for workers as well as their employers. One of the chief selling features for workers was that workers were vested immediately in the plans, which were portable. Traditional pension plans, to the contrary, often required that workers participate for at least ten years before they became eligible for any benefits. If they left a job before serving that amount of time, they would have nothing to show in future retirement benefits. With 401(k)s and similar plans, as long as the employee was a member of the plan, there would be something gained, no matter how brief the job. If employees had a series of short-term positions, they could in theory continually roll over the benefits and accumulate large enough portfolios to finance their retirements.

The immediate vesting and portability features seemed like advantages for me. I started my college teaching career in 1972, a particularly bad time to do so. The market was flooded with people who had similar credentials. Nearly across the board, colleges and universities were facing financial shortfalls. Far from adding new positions for people like me, they were looking for ways to cut back on teaching expenses while processing the same numbers of students.

Higher education administrators soon came up with a solution to their budget problems. They took advantage of the increasing availability of unemployed college teachers by employing them part-time on an ad hoc basis to teach courses at pay scales far lower than those of full-time faculty members. Within a decade, many colleges and universities were doing most of their teaching by employing part-time and temporary faculty members at bargain rates.

I spent the first thirteen years of my career as a member of this contingent university labor force in a series of part-time and temporary teaching positions. My number-one problem, especially after marrying and having children, was to find a secure teaching position. Worrying about retirement benefits was not my major concern. I was attracted to TIAA-CREF, a plan available at many colleges and universities. It was portable, so as you went from position to position—which was my experience—you could stay in the same plan. (Years later, I learned that the portability came at a very high cost of reduced retirement income.)

By the 1980s, when 401(k)s began to take off, their portability seemed made to order for the realities of most people's working lives. They needed plans that they could take with them from job to job. Of course, Social Security was such a plan, one of the reasons why it is so successful. But it was organized by the national government that had the resources and other capabilities to organize a truly national plan. Individual employers could have created a national organization so that their separate traditional pension plans would have been portable, but they did not. Instead, that became a selling point of the 401(k) industry.

Portability alone, though, would not have convinced workers that they were better off in a 401(k) than traditional pension plan. They had to believe that 401(k)s would provide more or at least the same amount of retirement income. If they had been told the truth at the time— that 401(k)s would provide less than half the retirement income—they would have resisted them. The financial services industry thus did all that it could to encourage the belief that 401(k)s would provide more generous benefits. It did that by projecting likely benefits using exceptionally optimistic assumptions of investment returns. Few, even very educated workers, knew enough to challenge those assumptions. Investing is after all a highly uncertain and complicated activity that relatively few people actively engage in. They usually leave it to others to figure out something so complicated.

The roaring stock market of 1990s seemed to confirm what the 401(k) promoters in the 1980s promised. Double-digit stock market and retirement account increases for many years made it look like investing was the easy road to retiring rich. Personal finance gurus like

Suze Orman, Dave Ramsey, and David Bach got into the game, urging and cajoling their followers to reduce spending on frivolities and invest their way to wealth as a moral obligation.[19] Financial firms, flush with cash, filled the media with advertisements promoting themselves as the responsible stewards of Americans' accumulating personal wealth.

As the 401(k) industry was taking off, I was bumping from job to job. At the end of 1978, I left San Francisco for a new teaching position at the University of Texas at El Paso. Unlike the position at San Francisco State, this was full-time and came with a choice of retirement plans. I could join the Teacher Retirement System (TRS) of Texas or TIAA-CREF. I knew next to nothing about retirement systems, but I had heard somewhere that TIAA was a retirement system designed for professors. It existed at most colleges and universities so that it was portable for faculty members who changed positions during their careers. I immediately chose TIAA and felt smug in the belief that I had made a shrewd decision.

TIAA-CREF was a defined contribution plan very much like the 401(k)s that were launched that year. It was in many ways the pioneer of the 401(k). In 1918, Andrew Carnegie contributed $1 million to start the Teachers Insurance and Annuity Association (TIAA) for college professors.[20] Carnegie undoubtedly thought that what was good enough for him was good enough for professors. If his security came from stock market investments, so could theirs. But, as I would later learn, there is a great difference between what a true capitalist like Carnegie can get out of the stock market and what someone of more modest means like me could get. Carnegie had much more money to invest than he needed for his personal living expenses, so he could easily endure stock market swings. They wouldn't have any impact on his present or future standard of living. College professors would find that market downswings could send them crashing into the ground.

I didn't give a thought to what a TIAA-CREF retirement income would be. I was in my thirties with several decades of work life ahead. If anything, I assumed that it would be good enough. After all, it was the plan of professors and surely they knew what they were doing, an assumption that I would learn much later was an illusion. I certainly was in no position to know that, in 2011, the Texas legislature would mandate a study that demonstrates that TRS members would do significantly worse if they were in a defined contribution plan like TIAA-CREF. The study showed that for a combined employer and employee contribution of 10.6 percent of salary, members of the TRS would receive a retirement income that would replace 68 percent of their preretirement income. Members of a self-directed, defined contribution plan like TIAA-CREF would receive only 28 percent of their preretirement incomes. The study also showed that to match the TRS retirement income based on a contribution rate of 10.6 percent of salary, contributions to a defined contribution plan would have to be 25.3 percent of salary—two-and-a-half times as much.[21]

A few months after settling into my job, a $542 check unexpectedly arrived in the mail from the California Public Employees' Retirement System. Unbeknownst to me, I had been a part of the state's defined benefit retirement system, though well short of vesting in it. The check was California's way of paying me off. For me, it was a windfall that I cashed without a second thought, and with that cashing went six years of meager retirement contributions.

Three years after starting my El Paso job, I was sitting in a Volkswagen repair shop waiting for my car. I overheard a well-dressed man explaining to the shop owner the wonders of 401(k)s and why he should set up one for his employees. "All of you will be able to save tax free for retirement," he said. "That's the beauty of it. You can't go wrong." At the time, I knew little about 401(k)s. I might have read something in the news about them, but the topic was far down my list of concerns.

I thought that the best type of retirement plan was a portable one that I could build up as I went from job to job. I had short-term positions. For all I knew, I would have short-term positions for my whole working life. I hoped that I would get long-term security somewhere, but I had no way of knowing whether that would happen. The 401(k) seemed like a TIAA approach for the whole country, which at that time seemed like a good idea to me.

My stay in El Paso ended unexpectedly after three and a half years. The day before the birth of my first daughter, I received a letter from the university authorities telling me that this would be my final year, with no explanation. All of my friends said it was politically motivated and shook their heads. My wife and I joked about naming our daughter "Pink Slip." I licked my wounds and prepared to move on.

The next stop was Lewis & Clark College in Portland, Oregon. The temporary full-time position was year to year. It also came with a retirement plan, but there was only one choice—TIAA-CREF. The University of Texas at El Paso had had two choices because it was linked into the state retirement system as well as contracted to TIAA-CREF. Lewis & Clark was a private college with no defined benefit pension system. I knew, though, that my days in Portland would be numbered because I did not have the security of a tenure track position. I kept searching.

Finally, in 1986, I found a position that was tenure track at Eastern Connecticut State University, a small liberal arts state university on the opposite coast. It carried the possibility of long-term stability. The reality of college teaching is that most people do not get tenure immediately after being employed. They go through a trial period of usually six years and then receive tenure if their employer decides to grant it. Tenure protects employees from being arbitrarily fired, as happened to me in El Paso. To fire someone, the employer has to have a defensible cause. I thus began this position like the previous ones, with no sense that I would be there for a long time. The only difference between my situation and that of most workers was that I had the hope of long-term security in the form of tenure—a precious advantage of teaching, if you can get it, over other types of work.

When I went to the human relations office, I had to sign a lot of papers. I chose a health-care plan provider and got keys to my office and a parking pass—all the things you get when starting a new job. There was that question of the retirement plan again. I had two choices: one was TIAA-CREF, which I'd had in El Paso and Portland, and the other was the state pension fund.

I still didn't know very much about the difference between the plans, and no one in the office explained them to me. I chose TIAA-CREF because I thought that it was consistent with what I had before and did not know how long I would last in this particular job. I might receive an offer of a position somewhere else. The state pension fund required ten years to fully vest. If I lost the job or went somewhere else before ten years was up, I would have nothing. TIAA-CREF vested immediately. I could take any contribution I had made with me if I left the job. That seemed to be another advantage.

Over time, especially when it looked as if I might be in the position for more years than I had expected, I began to wonder whether I had made the right decision. I then asked if I could change to the state pension plan and was told no. According to the rules, once an employee chose a retirement plan, it was an irrevocable decision. That bothered me at that time, as I still didn't know the real differences between the plans.

With my TIAA-CREF contract, I was in was the state's Alternate Retirement Program, a 401(a) that was very similar to the plan that the financial services industry salesman had been pitching to the El Paso VW repair shop owner. It was 1986, just five years after the beginning of the massive shift from guaranteed pensions to defined contribution 401(k) plans. True, mine wasn't a 401(k) as such, but the difference between the *k* and the *a* was a technicality that made no difference. The approach meant all of the risks of investing were mine with no guarantee that the plan would pay for a decent retirement at the end of my career. In place of a guaranteed result was only faith that the stock market would deliver.

CHAPTER 3

Army Tanks and Think Tanks

We were defeated by army tanks and think tanks.
—Naomi Klein, Annual Meeting,
American Sociological Association, 2007

On the morning of September 11, 1973, General Augusto Pinochet sent planes to bomb the national palace of Chile and then army tanks to surround it. By the end of the day, he had overthrown an elected civilian government. Salvador Allende, its socialist president, lay dead. Pinochet's military then murdered, tortured, and sent into exile thousands of Allende's supporters as it suspended democracy and established a right-wing military dictatorship that lasted until 1990.

"We won!" Sebastian Piñera cheered when he heard the news.[1] He and his brother, José, were economics graduate students at Harvard. He had reason to cheer. Because of the dictatorship's economic policies, he went on to become one of the wealthiest men in the world and then parlay part of that wealth to become president of Chile in 2009. His brother served the dictatorship directly as minister of labor and of mining. In the former post, he oversaw the first complete privatization of a public retirement system in history; in the latter post, he denationalized a substantial part of the copper industry. He was also instrumental in privatizing the electrical industry.

On that September morning in 1973, I was living in San Francisco. With horror, I followed the news as Allende supporters were rounded up into a soccer stadium where firing squads operated continually. In graduate school at the University of Wisconsin, I had known Chileans and Americans who were now in Chile and feared for their fates. Days after the coup, news came that two Americans I knew, Adam Schesch and Pat Schesch, were being held in the soccer stadium.

Robb McBride, a fellow student from the University of Wisconsin, and I decided to go to the Chilean consulate in San Francisco to express our concern for their safety. In the waiting room of the consulate, literature from the Allende government remained. The consular official received us cordially and indicated that he did not fully know what was happening in his country. Behind his worried look was the reality that he was a far-flung official who had already been cut off. In only a short time, he would become an exile like many others. Because many people were pressuring the dictatorship, the Schesches were released. A Chilean student I knew was also released after having received electric shocks to the genitals.

Two years later, I found myself living in an apartment with Chilean exiles in the Mission District of San Francisco. One exile, Elba Andrade, a schoolteacher, had endured terrible torture before being released into exile as a result of an Amnesty International campaign. Now in the United States, she needed to learn English. I wanted to get better at Spanish, a language that I had studied in college but still could not speak. We agreed to exchange language practice sessions. As a result, my Spanish improved enough to be able to teach it, which eventually led to the job in El Paso, where I was hired to teach sociology courses in Spanish to students coming across the border from Ciudad Juárez.

Shocked Chileans were living in a state of terror. The Pinochet regime, not just interested in ruling the country with an iron hand, strove to reverse all the economic and social policies of the previous left-wing government. Pinochet's advisers, called the "Chicago Boys" throughout Chile and Latin America, were products of Friedman's University of Chicago economics training program. They were apostles of his hyper-free market theories, championing, with the same fundamentalist faith of their mentor, a type of unfettered capitalism in which corporations and the rich were free to pursue their interests without government regulations.

PRIVATIZATION IN CHILE

The regime began by returning to their previous owners 250 state-owned companies that had been expropriated under the Allende government. Another 200 companies were sold off at low prices.[2] Then it carried out the most sweeping privatization in Latin American history, privatizing fully or partially 160 corporations, 16 banks, and some 3,600 agro-industrial plants and mines.[3] There were outright full privatizations when government-owned companies were sold, often at bargain basement prices and often via crony capitalism, to dictatorship-connected private interests.

The biggest prize was CODELCO, the national copper company. Chile holds 35 percent of the world's copper reserves, making copper the country's highest export earner.[4] Two American corporations, Anaconda and Kennecott, controlled most of the Chilean copper industry until 1971, when Allende began their nationalization. Pinochet confirmed the nationalization in 1976. Despite his international business-friendly attitude, he was aware of the importance of copper revenues for the future of the country. But nationalization contradicted neoliberal policy. José Piñera, then secretary of mining, took on the task of resolving that contradiction five years later in 1981. The nationalization could not be reversed for political reasons. He thus devised a law whereby CODELCO sold concessions to private companies to mine for copper with guaranteed generous indemnification in case of future expropriation. Piñera had found a way to expand private enterprise within the shell of state ownership. He wrote, "Chile's reform of its mining law could help other countries by demonstrating that there is a way to make the nominal state ownership that is written into several constitutions compatible with a robust property right over a 'full concession,' and thereby to open new fields for the creation of wealth through the activity of private entrepreneurs."[5] As a result, over 70 percent of the copper industry is now in private hands, including foreign, via the concessions.[6]

In a similar way, public schooling was substantially privatized. Before Pinochet, public schools were controlled by the national government with just a few private schools. In 1979, the dictatorship carried out two reforms. The first was to place schools under the control of municipalities. The second was to give public subsidies to private companies to provide schooling. These subsidized private schools turned out to be very profitable, largely because teachers' salaries were substantially lower than in public schools. They expanded rapidly. Between 1980 and 1987 in metropolitan Santiago de Chile, for example, the proportion of grade school students in subsidized private schools jumped from 22 percent to 47 percent.[7] Taxpayers provided the budgets, while private companies took the profits. The indirect privatization of public schooling in Chile and the issues of public and democratic control that it raises are similar to attempts to privatize public education in the United States with subsidized charter schools.

At the university level, privatization took another twist. The government dramatically reduced funding to public universities, forcing them to charge higher tuitions, placing greater debt burdens on students while providing a business boom for the financial services industry. Post-dictatorship governments did not reverse this trend. As a result, students reacted with massive demonstrations beginning in 2011 that shook the country. They demanded free tuition and an end to indirect privatization.

With so much privatization and expansion of competitive capitalism, a new culture based on fragmented individualism began to erode traditional Chilean values. When journalist Marta Harnecker returned to the country after seventeen years in exile in 1990, she found "another country. I had trouble recognizing it. I kept asking myself where was the Chile I had known. Solidarity among friends, among neighbors, among communities, so characteristic of our national idiosyncrasy, had disappeared. With a few exceptions, everybody was scrambling, concerned with survival in an increasingly competitive world."[8]

The centerpiece of the neoliberal transformation, carried out by José Piñera when he was secretary of labor and social security, was to completely privatize the national retirement system: to restructure it from one based on guaranteed pensions to one based on stock market investments in which there would be no guarantees. Friedman and Reagan imagined doing the same in the United States with Social Security, but they weren't positioned to carry out such a drastic elimination of the federal government's most popular and successful program. However, unlike the Reagan administration, when the military dictatorship took power in Chile without any democratic checks, it had absolute power to carry out whatever policies it wanted.

For Friedman and the Chicago Boys, the tragedy of Chile presented a great opportunity to put through the very reforms that they were unable to accomplish in societies where there was democratic participation. Eventually Friedman himself would advise the Chilean government. As Naomi Klein has persuasively argued in *The Shock Doctrine*, many of the regressive reforms of the past forty years have occurred in the aftermath of political or natural disasters in which corporate interests have taken advantage of those tragedies to put through the reforms they wanted, which they otherwise would have been unable to do.[9]

In Chile in 1981, the Chicago Boys overhauled the entire national retirement system from one based on guaranteed pensions to a new system based on investments. All new workers were required to join it. To fund the new system, called the *Administradoras de Fondos de Pensiones* or AFP, 12.5 percent of workers' salaries were deducted. There were no employer contributions, unlike in the old system. This change obviously made the new system very popular with employers. Business owners could open their own accounts for themselves. As an added incentive for rich business owners, they could invest as much of their money as they wanted in the accounts to avoid taxes. (After the dictatorship ended, limits were placed on how much could be invested.) For employees, individual accounts were opened and administered by private managers. Currently, Dutch multinational financial giant ING manages most accounts. But even with the power of a military dictatorship behind them, Piñera and the other Chicago Boys had to make accommodations. Those who were in the old system could remain in it, but any new worker had to go into the new system. As a way of convincing a wary public that the new system was in its interest, they guaranteed that in the event that people did not have enough to live above the poverty level when they retired, the government would make up the difference. The biggest accommodation was to the Chilean military; it was allowed to continue with a traditional pension system, in a tacit admission that retirement prospects would be worse under the new system.

In a 1988 plebiscite that the military set up with dubious democratic legitimacy and that Pinochet thought he would win handily, Chileans voted by a margin of fifty-six to forty-six against an eight-year extension of the dictatorship. That set in motion a two-year period of transition to the restoration of democratic elections in December 1989. By then, Pinochet's appalling human rights abuses had made him an international pariah, even to the United States government that had originally backed his coup d'état.

At the same time, many of Pinochet's mainstream international critics distinguished between his political and economic policies, condemning the former while tacitly praising the latter. It was too bad that Chile had to go through such a period of human rights abuses, they conceded, but at least the dictatorship had gotten the country's economic house in order. That distinction continued to be repeated in the business press long after the end of the dictatorship in 1990. When Pinochet died in 2006, the *Wall Street Journal*, *Business Week*, and *Forbes* strongly criticized his human rights abuses but praised his economic legacy.[10] According to the *Wall Street Journal*, his legacy improved with time. In 2013, commenting on turmoil in Egypt, the newspaper dropped reference to human rights issues and remembered Pinochet as an unblemished political as well as economic reformer: "Egyptians would be lucky if their new ruling generals turn out to be in the mold of Chile's Augusto Pinochet, who took power amid chaos but hired free-market reformers and midwifed a transition to democracy."[11] The reality, though, was that powerful economic interests had taken advantage of the dictatorship to push through reforms detrimental to ordinary Chileans that they never would have accomplished under democratic conditions, including, notably, to their retirement system.

THE WORLD BANK TAKES CHARGE

The only difference between what was wrought in Chile and what was developing in the United States with 401(k)s was the scale. Piñera and the Chicago Boys had eliminated the public retirement system in one swift move and replaced it with a mandatory private one. It was as if Social Security were eliminated as an option for all new employees, who would be required to have 401(k) accounts instead. But that difference pointed to the ultimate goals of neoliberals and the financial services industry: to capture all retirement savings, as had occurred in Chile. To get there, they would need more than the example provided by a military dictatorship in a small South American country. They needed a far more powerful source of influence, the World Bank.

The World Bank, created in 1944, was designed to be a banker for all countries worldwide. Donor countries contribute funds that it uses, in turn, to make loans to borrowing countries. Like any bank, it chooses which applicants—in this case, countries—to fund according to the worthiness of their applications and, at the same time, imposes conditions on the borrowers. Over time, the bank has accumulated enormous power and influence over the economic policies of poor countries. Not only is bank approval of the economic policies of countries necessary as a condition for receiving its loans, its seal of approval also functions as a rating of credit worthiness for receiving loans from other agencies.

In the course of elaborating its own loan policies, the bank also developed into a think tank for general development policy. It enters what it refers to as client countries and advocates reforms to a wide range of policies. In this context, it increasingly took notice of retirement systems in its client countries in the 1980s and began to advocate reforms. Since the mid-1980s, in the words of an official report, "support for pension reforms has become a significant and highly visible element of the Bank's activities."[12] Throughout, the bank has urged development of market-friendly retirement reforms.

In 1991, under the leadership of Lawrence Summers, its chief economist, its *World Development Report* presented its new market-friendly approach to retirement policy.[13] (Summers would go on to occupy key economic positions in the Clinton and Obama administrations, where he has also promoted market-friendly policies.) Later, in 1994, the bank further developed its strategy in another report, *Averting the Old Age Crisis*, which would establish an approach that hasn't fundamentally been changed since.

The bank took particular aim at "dominant public pillar" defined benefit, pay-as-you-go retirement systems as Chile had had. It argued that such systems were unsustainable largely because people were living longer. Further, "by giving governments control over a major share of the financial assets in a country, they deprive the private sector of access to these funds and thereby inhibit growth."[14] The bank argued that these systems, which existed mostly in Europe, should not be the models for developing countries.

While stressing that it was not prescribing a rigid approach, the bank nevertheless presented a "multipillar" system as the most sustainable and adequate. It should have three pillars: (1) a mandatory, publicly managed "means-tested minimum pension guarantee"; (2) a mandatory, privately managed defined contribution savings plan; and (3) a voluntary savings or occupational plan.[15]

At first glance, this looked like the traditional three-legged stool in the US system. But upon closer examination, there were radical differences. Unlike Social Security, in which benefits are determined by average earnings, benefits for the first pillar or leg would be "means tested." This program would be targeted to the poor rather than benefiting all working people. If administered in the United States, it would turn Social Security into a welfare program and thereby undercut its broad popular appeal. Whether there *should* be less public support for poverty-targeted programs than those that benefit all working people is another matter.

The second pillar contained an equally radical change. Rather than being composed of guaranteed defined benefits, as had been the case in the United States through 1980, it would be a mandatory, defined contribution national system. It would be similar to 401(k)s except that participation would be mandatory. This would provide the largest source of retirement income, according to the bank's prescription, and by being mandatory, would send more forced savings from workers into financial markets. The third pillar would be based on voluntary savings, as in the United States, or an employer-based plan.

The bank's prescription looked suspiciously more like what Piñera and the Chicago Boys had wrought in Chile than the traditional three-legged stool. As the most powerful international agency involved in shaping the future of retirement systems, its decision to endorse defined contribution systems sent a signal that was loud and clear, much more influential and effective than that of a right-wing military dictatorship. Piñera and the Chicago Boys had created a mandatory, national defined contribution system to replace the former defined benefit system. Unlike the Chileans, the bank avoided use of the politically charged term "privatization," as would President George W. Bush when he attempted a partial defined contribution reform of Social Security in 2005. But this was just a choice of terminology to describe what was the same in all important respects. Piñera's model also included the first pillar of a minimum guaranteed, publicly financed benefit to back up the privatized system.

The latest iteration of the bank's model now has four pillars:

1. A mandatory public system to provide a minimum guaranteed benefit as a safety net that would be available in the absence of other support. It could be a pay-as-you-go system with contributions based on earnings.
2. A mandatory, defined contribution plan to provide the largest fraction of retirement income.
3. Voluntary retirement savings, such as individual savings, or employment-based plans.
4. Nonfinancial benefits provided to the elderly, such as discounts on transportation and housing.[16]

The relationship between the first two mandatory pillars reveals the bank's approach to retirement reform. The first pillar, the public mandatory system, is to be a backup only for the second pillar, the mandatory, defined contribution system. National, public defined benefit pension systems that provide the bulk of retirement income are to be avoided in the construction of new systems and trimmed back in reforming existing ones. The greatest emphasis is placed on developing the second pillar of defined contribution systems.

THE CHILEAN MODEL GOES INTERNATIONAL

In the 1990s, the World Bank urged other Latin American countries to follow the Chilean example, with varying degrees of success. Despite widespread popular opposition, by 2003 eleven other countries had completely or partially privatized their social security systems—Peru (1992), Colombia (1993), Argentina (1994), Uruguay (1996), Mexico (1997), El Salvador (1997), Bolivia (1998), Costa Rica (2000), Nicaragua (2000), Ecuador (2001), and the Dominican Republic (2003). Major countries that rejected the World Bank prescription altogether included Brazil, the largest in Latin America, and the Bolivarian Republic of Venezuela.

Privatization of Mexico's social security system was particularly egregious. For context, we have to go back to the presidential election of 1988, which came after a period of serious economic stagnation—called by many the lost decade. The *Partido Revolucionario Institucion* (PRI), which had exercised near dictatorial control over the country for six decades, was facing probable defeat at the polls. On July 6, election night, the first results showed the opposition candidate, Cuauhtemoc Cárdenas, headed for a sweeping victory. Then came a mysterious breakdown of the computers reporting votes. No further results were announced for twenty-four hours. When announcement of the results resumed, the PRI's candidate, Carlos Salinas de Gortari, was taking the lead and was declared the winner.

Because Cárdenas represented the Mexican Left, the Reagan administration did not criticize the obvious fraud. It had bigger plans for the country that Cárdenas would have opposed. In 1988, the United States and Canada had signed a free trade agreement. The intention was to expand it to Mexico.

Free trade agreements represent the embodiment of neoliberal ideology taken from the domestic to the international arena. Domestically, proponents of neoliberal reforms such as Friedman successfully sought to free up market transactions by removing government regulations, hence, the widespread deregulation of American industry in past decades. The next step was to remove government regulations of international trade, which were exercised mainly through tariffs for imported goods. According to free market advocates, removal of tariffs would increase trade, economic growth, and competition. Inefficient industries that had been protected by national high tariff walls would either have to become more competitive or go out of business.

The counterargument, though, is that free trade agreements magnify the power of the strong over the weak. They make it easier for corporations to move factories to low-wage areas in other countries. Economically weaker countries are no longer able to use tariffs to protect developing industries from the cheap imports of foreign, more developed industries (as had been a policy practiced by the United States during the nineteenth century to protect its industries from imports from the more powerful British economy). In the case of Mexico, millions of peasant farmers faced potential economic extinction if US agribusiness corporations could flood their traditional markets with tariff-free surplus corn produced under lower-cost industrial conditions, as they did. That, in turn, would force them off the land and into the cities and migration stream to the United States, as did occur.[17]

The first public confirmation of the rumored plans for what was to become the North American Free Trade Agreement (NAFTA) was made in the spring of 1990. At the same time, I learned that I had received a Fulbright grant for research and teaching at Latin America's largest university, the venerable Universidad Nacional Autónoma de México (UNAM) in Mexico City. (I did not know at the time that I would be working in the same building as Orlando Caputo, the man in charge of copper nationalization under Allende and now in exile.)

When I arrived in Mexico City that summer, there was a climate of expectation about what NAFTA would bring. Unlike in Canada and the United States, where it was provoking large public debates over trade policy, in Mexico there was controlled optimism. NAFTA would solve all the country's economic problems. Newspapers ran headlines such as "Within Five Years of NAFTA, Mexican Wages Will Equal Those of the United States" and "With NAFTA Mexico Will Leave the Third World." I was clearly living in a party dictatorship. When the ruling party made a decision, all of its political representatives and the major media fell in line. There were exceptions such as the left-wing daily, *La Jornada*, but they were rare.

The year 1990 was just after the fall of the Berlin Wall and just before the 1991 dissolution of Cold War arch nemesis, the Soviet Union. That summer as I took up residency in Mexico City, John Negroponte was taking over as US ambassador to Mexico. Negroponte may be the most controversial diplomat in the recent history of the US State Department. He began his career in Vietnam and then oversaw the embassy in Honduras during the height of the Contra War in neighboring Nicaragua. After his Mexican posting, he sat out the eight years of the Clinton presidency. Republican President George W. Bush brought him back to be ambassador to the United Nations. If the September 11, 2001, terrorist attacks had not happened, the Senate would likely not have confirmed his appointment because of allegations of human rights misconduct during the Honduras ambassadorship. But after the September 11 attack, the Senate was in no mood to delay appointments. After the UN posting, he became ambassador to occupied Iraq and later had the posts of director of national intelligence and deputy secretary of state.

Because Mexico is a large border country, it has high strategic importance for US foreign policy. The US embassy in Mexico City has at times been its largest one in the world. Appointments to the ambassadorship are not made lightly. But even by those standards, Negroponte was an unusually heavyweight appointment. He had been the ambassador to impoverished, sparsely populated Honduras because it was in the center of the Central American wars in the 1980s with El Salvador to its north and Nicaragua to its south, which the United States sought to control. Now he was in Mexico to do an equally important job: to ensure that Mexican officials cooperated with the NAFTA project. Mexican officials from the PRI, after some initial misgivings about such an asymmetrical arrangement, did cooperate. Passage of NAFTA, while in doubt in Canada and the United States, was never questioned in Mexico, where the PRI had dictatorial control over political decision making.

NAFTA opened the country to foreign imports and investments. In one fell swoop, it effected a neoliberal transformation of what had been a protected economy. What a military dictatorship had done in Chile, a party dictatorship did in Mexico. On January 1, 1994, NAFTA went into effect. There were immediate problems. The Zapatista National Liberation Army, named after the iconic leader of the Mexican Revolution and comprising Indians from the impoverished southern state of Chiapas, intentionally chose that day to launch a short-lived armed attempt to overthrow the Mexican government. It stated that it had picked that day because NAFTA would further impoverish Indians. That year also saw several high-profile political assassinations, including that of Luis Donaldo Colosio, the PRI's candidate in the coming presidential election. In December 1994, the peso spectacularly crashed. It had been artificially overvalued during the lead-up to passage of NAFTA, some believe intentionally so in order to create a public climate favorable to passage. The day of reckoning came and the economy took a nosedive.

This shock to the economy presented a new opportunity for the neoliberal transformation of the country. As Friedman argued, crisis presents opportunity. In an atmosphere of desperation to do something about the obvious economic crisis that had people reeling, radical free-market policies could be proposed and enacted as either bold solutions or bitter but necessary medicine. Ernesto Zedillo was now president in unenviable economic circumstances, and there were fissures within the PRI. But the party was still in dictatorial control. It had disciplined majorities in both chambers of the legislature. NAFTA, it turned out, would be only act one of a two-act neoliberal transformation.

PRI officials, with advisers from Chile and the World Bank, argued that the country's economic crisis was being aggravated by its public pension system. As in Chile, the system had to be privatized, and it was. In December 1995, the government presented a legislative proposal for complete privatization and *within one month* obtained its passage with enactment in 1997. It was the most sweeping Latin American public pension privatization since the 1981 Chilean precedent. In an important respect, it was even more significant than the precedent. It was occurring in a country whose population was over seven times as large, resulting in seven times as much new business for the private financial services industry.

As in Chile, there was no necessary fiscal reason to privatize the Mexican pension system. Its problems could have been resolved with reforms such as increased contribution rates that would have retained its defined benefit basis. But the architects of pension privatization were not interested in reforms to shore up the old system. They wanted to destroy the old system to make way for a new one that was more compatible with their notion of the logic of a free enterprise system. As in Chile, the privatization required a government that, if not overtly dictatorial, was equally able to operate without any democratic checks on its power.

A NEW FRONTIER FOR PRIVATIZATION

The simultaneous collapse of communist control in Central and Eastern Europe opened up a second front for retirement privatization in the 1990s. Retirement systems under the communists had been public and pay-as-you-go, with generous benefits and low retirement ages. In some cases, there was no separation between pension and national budgets. One could be critical of the communist systems, but they delivered retirement security. That level of retirement security would not emerge unscathed as free market reformers undid the old economic systems.

The financial services industry with the World Bank as its tacit leader had found a new frontier after Latin America. It had found it somewhat unexpectedly, since few people in the early 1980s, when

401(k)s and privatization of national retirement systems began, had predicted such a quick and thorough demise of the communist systems that had seemed so entrenched. Regardless, it was a tremendous opportunity for private retirement provision expansion and was recognized as such.

Unlike the United States where occupational retirement plans are supposed to provide the bulk of retirement income, national retirement systems inherited from the communist periods provided virtually all of retirement income, with all contributions and benefits flowing through government budgets. Following the World Bank recipe, the key task was to divert as much as possible to private financial channels. A major obstacle, though, was that Western European countries generally also had traditional, dominant, public pension pillars that enjoyed strong public support, even more than Social Security in the United States. Eastern Europeans were more likely to look west on their own continent than south and across an ocean to Chile for retirement reform models. In the case of Poland, the World Bank and the US Agency for International Development attempted to overcome this reluctance by sponsoring a trip to Chile for members of parliament, social security experts, and journalists.[18] They made sure that journalists were along, expecting them to send back glowing stories about the Chilean system to soften expected public opposition to pension privatization.

The ideal, from the World Bank's neoliberal point of view, was to make a private defined contribution system not just available but the main pillar of support. But, as in Latin America, ex-communist countries varied greatly in how close they came to the bank's ultimate goal. Kazakhstan came the closest.[19] The Czech Republic and Slovenia resisted the most by keeping reformed versions of their traditional defined benefit systems. Private accounts were instituted but only as voluntary supplements. As for what would happen to retirees under the old system or to older workers who had built up substantial credits, most of the new governments bowed to expediency and allowed them to keep their relatively generous benefits, while subjecting younger workers to the reforms. Others devised schemes to transfer credits from the old to new systems. One of the strange results of this, as we shall see, is that current retirees are secure because of their benefits from the old systems. There is no retirement crisis—yet. That will happen in around 2040 when those who were twenty in 1995 reach sixty-five. The effect will be delayed, as it was in Chile and the United States.

Four countries (Poland, Mongolia, Latvia, and the Kyrgyz Republic) changed from defined benefit to *notional*, defined contribution, national retirement systems. This new model first emerged in Italy in 1995. In it, as in any defined contribution program, workers make contributions, with their benefits determined by the size of their accumulations. But unlike 401(k) and most other defined contribution plans, their contributions are not invested. Rather, they go into a government fund from which benefits are paid—on a pay-as-you-go basis. Individuals have accounts in their names, but these are "notional" accounts, that is, as an accounting device only. The government tracks how much an individual contributes and adds to it values determined by the country's growth rate. The formula for determining benefits is based on the size of the notional accumulation.

The World Bank cried foul. That was not the type of retirement reform it had in mind. Notional defined contribution plans did not divert retirement funds from government to private ones for stock market investments. They created no new sources of accumulation for private capital. In a policy briefing, it bluntly stated that "they are not an adequate substitute for a funded system based on a true defined-contribution pension" and approvingly quoted Olivia Mitchell, a Wharton business professor, who described them as "an unfunded defined benefit plan in defined contribution sheep's clothing."[20]

Russia, the largest of the countries, adopted a mixed model in 2001 that fell far short of the World Bank's ideal of a dominant private pillar. The new system has three pillars of different sizes. Half of retirement contributions finance a public flat-rate pension. Another 28.6 percent of contributions finance notional defined contribution plan funds that also operate in the public sector. The remainder of retirement contributions—21.4 percent—goes into newly established private accounts.[21]

How well do World Bank officials follow their prescriptions for the rest of the world with their own retirement plan? Not very. The bank's very generous staff retirement plan has three tiers. The first is a defined benefit—yes, *defined benefit*—plan that includes a cost-of-living adjustment (COLA). The benefit formula is the number of years worked times 1 percent times final salary. The second tier is a defined contribution plan for which the bank contributes an unusually high 10 percent of salary and employees contribute 5 percent. The final tier is a voluntary tax-deferred savings plan based on employee contributions.[22] If that isn't enough, employees in the Washington, DC, headquarters have an additional 401(k) plan so that altogether they can place up to $49,000 of their annual incomes in retirement savings that are shielded from taxation.[23] This last benefit is most useful to the bank's highest-paid officials who have much more disposable income than immediate living expenses. American employees of the World Bank are also covered by Social Security.

Social Security and the defined benefit first tier of the pension plan provide more than half of salary replacement for most World Bank employees. This would seem to violate the bank's prescription that the bulk of income should come from defined contribution private accounts. If the bank was true to its principles, it would have no defined benefit component for its employees in the United States since their Social Security coverage would be more than adequate to guard them against elderly poverty. In fairness, the latest iteration of the bank's global retirement prescription allows for "voluntary" employer defined benefit plans in its third pillar. The bank's defined benefit component, though, covers all employees and is therefore not voluntary. More important is that the bank's prescription for others carries the clear implication that defined benefit plans should have no more than a marginal role in benefit provision, while that is not the case for its own plan. It appears to have learned from the Chilean military the importance of hedging its bets on the supposed superiority of private defined contribution plans by providing a defined benefit pension backup for itself.

CHAPTER 4

Targeting Social Security and Public Worker Pensions

On the eve of the Reagan presidency in 1980, Milton and Rose Friedman published *Free to Choose*, a proposal for gradually phasing out Social Security. The entitlements of retirees would be honored as would the accumulated credits of contributors who had not yet retired. But no new payroll taxes would be collected. The final elimination of Social Security would allow "individuals to provide for their own retirement as they wish." Among the advantages would be that "it would add to personal saving and so lead to a higher rate of capital formation [and] stimulate the development and expansion of private pension plans."[1] While the Friedmans argued for such a plan, they acknowledged that immediate privatization of retirement was unrealistic in the current political climate, but they would accept incremental reforms with the hope that one day total privatization would become politically feasible.

That same year, the conservative Koch brothers-financed Cato Institute published *Social Security: The Inherent Contradiction*, by Peter Ferrara, which argued that instead of being required to participate in Social Security, people should "be allowed to choose from a variety of insurance and investment options offered in the private market."[2] The previous year, two years after its founding in 1977, the institute had published an article by Carolyn Weaver in which she made the case for privatization, and in 1980 it also sponsored a conference on Social

Security privatization that drew, among others, two hundred congressional staffers.

When Ronald Reagan came into office in 1981, Social Security was facing a shortfall in revenue necessary to meet expenses. Reforms of some type were necessary. Privatization, while undoubtedly attractive to Reagan and his inner circle, was not politically feasible. It was a new idea that still had not gained traction in the governing class, and the United States was not Chile, with a military dictatorship that could impose it by fiat. Social Security would have to be reformed by raising taxes or lowering benefits, or some combination of the two to bring its budget back into balance. Increasing the then contribution rate of 5.35 percent would be a tax rise that was anathema to Reagan's conservative principles. Instead, there would have to be benefit reductions.

Reagan had appointed David A. Stockman, an advocate of neoliberal economics, as his director of the Office of Management and Budget and charged him with reducing welfare entitlements. Stockman soon turned to the problem of Social Security, which he described as "one giant Ponzi scheme." What particularly bothered him was its intentionally redistributional feature wherein lower-income groups received greater returns on their contributions than higher-income ones to keep them out of poverty. This he saw as "closet socialism," an unearned welfare benefit.[3] His planned cuts were announced in May 1981. The main cut reduced benefits of those who retired early at age sixty-two before their age of full retirement at sixty-five. Their benefits would be slashed from 80 percent to 55 percent of full retirement age benefits.[4] Negative reaction was immediate from senior groups, labor unions, and politicians. The Senate passed a 96–to-0 motion in opposition.

Facing such a firestorm of opposition, the Reagan administration retreated and regrouped. It then chose a different and less confrontational course of action. In 1983, the president named a commission with Alan Greenspan at its head to devise internal reforms for Social Security financing. As a result of Greenspan Commission recommendations, reforms were made to both increase revenues and decrease benefits—the first benefit decreases in the history of Social Security. It was a compromise. Reagan had to accept a tax increase that would rise to 6.2 percent that he did not want. Supporters of Social Security had to accept benefit cuts that they did not want.

The main reduction of benefits came from a gradual increase in the normal retirement age from sixty-five at the inception of the program in 1935 to sixty-seven for workers born after 1960. The more that retirement was delayed, the less that the fund would have to pay out in benefits.

Social Security benefits had not previously been taxed, but beginning in 1984, they would be partially taxed. The reform established two income thresholds that would be adjusted according to inflation and other causes. Recipients whose combined income from all sources falls below the first threshold do not have any of their Social Security income subject to taxes. Those between that and the top threshold have 50 percent of Social Security benefits counted as income for tax purposes, while those above the top threshold have 85 percent counted. Taxation of benefit income increases Social Security revenues because it is kept within the program, though it decreases benefit amounts for those subject to it.

Additionally, the Windfall Elimination Provision (WEP), also implemented in 1984, reduced the benefits of individuals with long periods of uncovered employment. Social Security officials had noticed in benefit calculations that such individuals appeared to be poorer than they really were and therefore eligible for higher income replacement amounts. Social Security was in part designed as an elderly poverty prevention program. The poor receive higher income replacements than those with higher incomes. If a person had twenty years of covered and thirty years of uncovered employment, the thirty years of zero contributions were treated as thirty years of zero income. That pulled down the overall income average to below poverty levels, making them eligible for higher benefit amounts than they otherwise would have been.

The WEP eliminated the extra income. But it did it in an awkward manner that caused hardship for those subject to it. In its annual statement of estimated benefits, Social Security does not take into account any possible impact of the WEP. It only states that there could be an impact on some individuals. That leads individuals subject to the provision to believe that their benefits will be higher than they actually will be.

A LENINIST STRATEGY

Privatization advocates were not happy that the system was only being internally reformed and never abandoned their long-range goal. In 1984, the year that the Greenspan reforms began, Stuart Butler and Peter Germanis from the Heritage Foundation wrote "Achieving a 'Leninist' Strategy," a plan for waging "guerrilla warfare against the Social Security System and the coalition that supports it," which was published in the *Cato Journal*.[5] Their nod to Vladimir Lenin, the architect of the Bolshevik Revolution, who is not normally approvingly cited in conservative literature, was based on an analogy. In the authors' understanding, Lenin viewed capitalism as an unstable system that would eventually collapse because of its inherent contradictions. To speed up the collapse, it was necessary to mobilize workers and others who would gain from the future socialist society.

Butler and Germanis, as free market conservatives, did not agree that capitalism was doomed to collapse from its internal contradictions or that workers would be better served under socialism. They believed that it was Social Security by way of analogy that was doomed because of its contradictions, and its collapse could be speeded up through political organizing. What they were really interested in borrowing from Lenin was his shrewd organizing skill. Lenin understood, according to Butler and Germanis, "that fundamental change is contingent both upon a movement's ability to create a focused political coalition and upon its success in isolating and weakening its opponents."[6] The key was to divide the coalition in favor of maintaining Social Security while mobilizing a coalition that would supposedly gain from private accounts. The first step would be to neutralize opposition to privatization from present beneficiaries by assuring them that their benefits

would be maintained—a tactic employed in many occupational benefit conversions to less favorable plans. The reform would only affect
younger workers, who needed to be educated about the problems of
Social Security and how they would be supposedly better served by
private accounts. "An economic education campaign . . . must be un-
dertaken to demonstrate the weaknesses of the existing system and to
allow it to be compared accurately (and therefore unfavorably) with
the private alternative."[7] Who should carry out this "education" campaign? None other than the main beneficiaries of privatization, who
Butler and Germanis unabashedly identified as "the banks, insurance
companies, and other institutions that will gain from providing such
plans to the public."[8]

It's not difficult to see why Butler and Germanis thought that the
financial services industry would be interested in Social Security privatization. Thirty-five percent of total retirement contributions in the
United States are made to Social Security, which puts them beyond
the reach of the private market.[9] The more that Social Security can
be privatized, the more new profit opportunities the financial services
industry will have. If it cannot be privatized immediately, the more that
its benefits can be reduced, the more that people will have to resort to
private accounts for their retirement provision. That economic interest
is completely consistent with the conservative think tanks' traditional
promotion of the free enterprise system. The current *Cato Handbook
for Policymakers* lists as a key talking point that workers would do significantly better with private accounts than Social Security.[10]

> Social Security taxes are already so high, relative to benefits, that
> Social Security has quite simply become a bad deal for younger
> workers, providing a low, below-market rate of return. This poor
> rate of return means that many young workers' retirement ben-
> efits are far lower than if they had been able to invest those
> funds privately. However, a system of individual accounts, based
> on private capital investment, would provide most workers with

significantly higher returns. Those higher returns would translate into higher retirement benefits, leading to a more secure retirement for millions of seniors.[11]

That claim is consistent with the "Leninist" strategy first announced thirty years ago: assure those in or near retirement that their benefits won't change, while convincing younger workers that they would be better off in a new privatized system. After leaving office, George W. Bush continued to repeat the claim that private accounts would deliver better returns than Social Security. In his 2010 memoir, *Decision Points*, he stated, "Younger workers should have the option of earning a better return by investing part of their Social Security taxes in personal retirement accounts."[12]

COMPARISON OF SOCIAL SECURITY AND PRIVATE PLANS

Is it true that private accounts deliver higher rates of return than Social Security? To test the claim, I started by comparing my Social Security statement with my TIAA-CREF statement. Both list the total contributions made by employers and me. The Social Security statement indicates my benefit at sixty-six, the age of my full retirement. My TIAA-CREF statement has the total accumulation. Since I was nearly sixty-six, I knew how much an annuity income it was worth. My first-year Social Security benefit was 12.61 percent of my total contributions. The first-year TIAA annuity was 12.06 of total contributions—*lower*, not higher than the return on my Social Security contributions as the Cato Institute and President Bush so confidently claimed. Remember also that as a professional, I am in a relatively high-income category with a Social Security rate of return that is less than that of lower-income participants. For them, the rate of return for Social Security compared to private accounts would be much higher than mine, making it an even better deal. On top of that, Social Security contains disability insurance for all income groups, while private plans do not.

Former Secretary of the Treasury Lawrence Summers, despite his being associated with privatization plans, gave one reason why Social Security's rate of return compares favorably with private plans: "Social Security is effective, in large part because it is efficient. More than 99 cents are paid in benefits by Social Security for every dollar that is paid in by workers and employers. Few, if any, private systems—anywhere in the world—come close to matching this efficiency."[13]

Like the optimistic projections of the financial services industry whose interests it serves, the Cato Institute's claim is based on before-the-fact, overly optimistic assumptions of future market returns. My comparison was based on after-the-fact, actual experience.

Butler and Germanis, in their strategy of undermining public support, had called for requiring Social Security to send annual statements of accounts to participants. Individuals could then compare their returns from private investment with their returns under Social Security. Younger workers would see just how much of a loss they are supposedly taking by participating in the program. This mechanism for demonstrating the individual gains and losses that occur under Social Security would be a key step in weakening public support for the present system.[14]

A PUSH FOR PRIVATIZATION

In 1989, New York Senator Daniel Patrick Moynihan, a supporter of private accounts, sponsored an amendment to the Social Security Act to require that such statements be sent to participants—the origin of the current Social Security statement that began in 1995.[15] If the motive behind the legislation was to promote support for private accounts over Social Security, it has backfired, as the statements have helped people to realize the value of the program, especially during stock market declines.

Through the end of the 1980s, the campaign for Social Security privatization remained ideological. The financial services industry was content with its burgeoning 401(k) business, and there were no serious legislative proposals on the table. The trust fund itself, following the 1984 revenue increases, had a growing surplus, but that didn't stop the conservative think tanks from attempting to undermine public confidence in it.

The 1994 publication of the World Bank's *Averting the Old Age Crisis* lent needed legitimacy to the privatization crusade to move it into mainstream political support. The implication of the bank's privatization manifesto was that most of Social Security should be replaced by mandatory private accounts, leaving only a small part of the original system to mitigate elderly poverty. That same year, a Social Security advisory commission released a report that included the recommendations of privatization advocates.

The privatization campaign regained traction. Republicans, as always, were warm to privatization proposals, but now with World Bank approval, so-called "New" and "Third Way" Democrats that included President Bill Clinton joined the campaign. Prominent Democrats who favored some form of privatization included Summers; Jeffrey Sachs, a major adviser on the Russian privatization reforms; Bob Kerrey, a senator from Nebraska; and Joseph Lieberman, a senator from Connecticut who was the party's 2000 vice presidential candidate.

This was the first fissure in the Democratic Party's traditional stalwart defense of Social Security, the crown jewel of New Deal social programs. The fissure revealed the growing momentum of the privatization coalition; the idea had moved from the ideological sidelines to embrace by the financial services industry as a new goal. The financial services industry, through its campaign contributions and lobbyists, had influence within the Democratic as well Republican parties. A fifth column had opened up among the party's elites. The Democrat privatizers, though, had even greater political problems than the Republican ones. They didn't have to just worry about passing an unpopular proposal over widespread public opposition. Unlike the Republicans, they also had to deal with widespread objections from their own party's base, especially labor unions, and other members of their elite as well. Clinton's support, though, of NAFTA and welfare reform had indicated that he was willing to defy the opposition of his party's base when he thought it was necessary because of economic pressure from elites, as in the case of NAFTA, or political expediency, as in the case of welfare reform.

From the ideological sidelines, Friedman continued to urge privatization. Meanwhile, the Cato Institute offered as its expert to head a Social Security privatization project none other than José Piñera, the former minister of labor of the Pinochet dictatorship who was responsible for completely privatizing Chile's national retirement system. After the return of democracy, Piñera had run for president in 1993. The Chilean people rewarded him for his service to the dictatorship with 6 percent of the vote. He then moved to Washington to continue his privatization mission from the more hospitable corridors of the Cato Institute. Piñera has had his eyes on more than US Social Security since leaving Chile. He has been on a mission to promote pension privatization throughout the world, following the model he designed and implemented in Chile. There is probably no single name as attached to its promotion as his. He claims that he lives on airplanes in an endless quest to spread the gospel of pension privatization. His website contains a color-coded international map titled "Atlas Freed," after conservative icon Ayn Rand's best-selling novel *Atlas Shrugged.* The map purports to show in red the spread of the Chilean privatization model that he inaugurated, reminiscent in an obverse way of 1950s Cold War maps that showed the spread of the red tide of communism.

By the end of the 1990s, the most prominent conservative think tanks—Heritage, American Enterprise Institute, Cato, Manhattan— were often considered to be mainstream noncontroversial sources of information for newspaper and television reports about retirement issues. A 1998 Fairness and Accuracy in Reporting study found that conservative think tanks were often cited in media stories without identifying them as conservative. On the other hand, when liberal think tanks were cited, they were more often labeled as left or left leaning, making their findings ideologically suspect.[16]

As of 1998, prospects for some form of Social Security privatization with Bill Clinton at the helm looked promising. Reportedly, a secret White House group worked on a partial privatization proposal for eighteen months.[17] But after the Monica Lewinsky scandal exploded, the president backed away from launching any new initiatives that were likely to meet widespread public opposition.[18] After the turnabout, historian Robin Blackburn wrote the wryly titled "How Monica Lewinsky Saved Social Security."[19]

What emerged instead was a rhetorical campaign to put what was then a growing federal revenue surplus into a "lock box" to "Save Social Security First."[20] Appended to the proposal was a provision to create USA accounts in which citizens could contribute up to $1,000 a year with an equal federal match into private accounts.

In the 2000 presidential election campaign, Republican and Democratic candidates George W. Bush and Al Gore presented different "carve-out" and "add-on" partial privatization proposals for Social Security. A carve-out would divert existing revenue into private accounts. An add-on proposal, like the USA accounts, would continue the same revenue base for Social Security, while giving citizens government subsidies to open private accounts in addition.

Carve-outs create tremendous transition costs for pay-as-you-go systems since revenue streams are reduced, while obligations are still in force. Add-ons avoid that problem but choke off the possibility of expanding the defined benefit character of Social Security. They represent a virtual commitment to all future government involvement in retirement provision on a defined contribution basis that subsidizes private accounts.

During his first term in office, President Bush laid the groundwork for partial privatization. His appointed disingenuously titled Commission to Strengthen Social Security issued its report in December 2001: "Strengthening Social Security and Creating Personal Wealth for All Americans." After winning reelection in 2004, the carve-out privatization proposal in the report became his top domestic priority. In January 2005, Karl Rove and Ken Mehlman designed a campaign to win public support for the reform. Two weeks later in the State of the Union address, the president announced his proposal, stating that Social Security was in crisis.

Under the plan, which would have been voluntary, individuals would have been able to divert 4 percent of the 12.4 percent Social Security payroll tax up to a limit of $1,000 a year to private individual accounts. That would have resulted in a carve-out and diversion of about 16 percent of Social Security revenues. Although the president insinuated that benefits would increase under the proposal, according to a Congressional Budget Office analysis, those opting for the individual accounts would suffer significant losses. Wage replacement rates for low-income workers would drop from 70 to 44 percent, for middle-income workers from 40 to 22 percent, and for high-income workers from 23 to 13 percent.[21] Diversion of 16 percent of revenues would also have created enormous transition costs for the new system that could have only been made up with benefits cuts, a bailout from other federal revenues, or some combination of the two.

Bush toured the country to sell the idea and garner public support, but it quickly became evident that people weren't buying. The more he tried to sell the proposal, the more opposed public opinion became. Between January and June 2005, the Gallop Poll indicated that opposition to the proposal had risen from 48 to 64 percent.[22] A coalition of organizations opposed to the proposal, which included labor unions and organizations of retired people, mounted an impressive counter-campaign. In a rare show of unity, almost all Democratic members of Congress were opposed. By late summer, the president was forced to abandon the proposal.

The partial privatization campaign ran into strong public opposition because so much of the public tangibly benefits from Social Security. It covers 94 percent of the labor force and replaces a substantial amount of preretirement income for most participants, keeping much of the elderly population out of poverty. Without it, 45.2 percent of the elderly population would be in poverty compared to the actual rate of 9.7 percent. Social Security benefits keep over 13 million elderly people out of poverty.[23] That feature alone wins support from younger persons who benefit indirectly because the existence of Social Security spares them from financially supporting older relatives.

The origin of the description of Social Security as the third rail of American politics resides in the statistical fact that sixty-five and older voters have the highest participation rate in elections. In the 2006 midterm election, for example, 60.5 percent of sixty-five and older persons voted, much higher than the 54.3 percent of the next highest group, those from forty-five to sixty-four years old. Put differently, those sixty-five and older made up 22.5 percent of the electorate, even though they are only 16.2 percent of the voting age population. Altogether, the forty-five and older population that includes the retired and those approaching retirement made up nearly two-thirds of voters.[24]

A NEW BENEFIT-REDUCTIONS CAMPAIGN

The Bush proposal was defeated despite being launched when the stock market was modestly recovering following the September 11, 2001, terrorist attacks. That would seem to have put the issue to rest, especially after the 2008 plunge in market and 401(k) values. Though chastened by the resounding political defeat of Bush's partial privatization proposal, the opponents of Social Security reluctantly regrouped around a plan B approach to reduce its benefits, as had occurred under the Reagan administration. This was in line with the World Bank campaign to reduce public pillars in overall retirement provision. In 2010, President Barack Obama, with Summers as his director of the National Economic Council, appointed a supposedly bipartisan National Commission of Fiscal Responsibility and Reform charged with developing proposals to reduce the national deficit. He loaded the commission with Social Security opponents.

By the end of the year, as expected, the chairpersons of the commission, Erskine Bowles, a Democrat, and Alan Simpson, a Republican, announced proposals that included broad cuts to Social Security benefits.

Simpson had earlier revealed his views crudely when he described Social Security, in an e-mail to the executive director of the national Older Women's League, as "like a milk cow with 310 million tits."[25]

Bowles and Simpson proposed raising the full retirement age to sixty-nine, up from the increase to sixty-seven established by the Greenspan Commission in 1984. The rationale was that improved health conditions have led people to live longer. The longer that people live in retirement, the more that has to be paid to them in benefits, placing pressure on the fund. Improved health conditions presumably also make workers capable of working longer.

The problem with this assumption, as with all attempts to fix unitary retirement ages, is that working capabilities vary among individuals according to their own states of health and the nature of their jobs. Mining and construction wear out workers faster than teaching and administration. According to one study, 27 percent of workers age fifty-eight or older perform physically demanding jobs that cause them to age faster than those with less physically demanding ones. Another 18 percent perform jobs in difficult working conditions that also place strains on their health. Not surprisingly, there is a general correlation between income and being spared from performing physically demanding, damaging jobs. The higher the income of workers and employees, the less likely they are to have physically demanding jobs.[26] Social class, in other words, is involved in selecting whose working conditions allow them to work and live longer. Longevity, it follows, has not increased across the board for all income groups. It has increased most for high-income groups, with low-income groups showing little increase. According to a careful study of Social Security records, life expectancy increased for all babies born between 1912 and 1941. But it increased far more for those in the top half of the earnings distribution. For them, it increased by an average 6 years compared to 1.3 years for those in the bottom half.[27] To delay when low-income groups, who also tend to have the most physically demanding jobs, can retire is to make them disproportionately pay the cost of higher-income groups living longer.

Bowles and Simpson proposed reducing the annual cost-of-living adjustment (COLA). Reducing COLAs would squeeze elderly budgets when medical costs usually rise. In the same way that inflation erodes the buying power of those on fixed incomes over time, reducing COLAs would reduce buying power by increasing the gap between annual benefit and actual cost-of-living increases.

By far the most significant but least obvious proposal—one that was rarely mentioned in press accounts—was to change the formula for determining benefits. Bowles and Simpson proposed changing it so that benefits would be shifted from higher- to lower-income groups. On the surface, this would appear to be a progressive policy—and they used the word *progressive* intentionally in their proposal to at least rhetorically appeal for liberal support—but it was deceptive. The effect of the formula change would reduce the benefits of middle-class participants by as much as 36 percent, thereby undermining their politically critical support for the program.[28] The long-term effect, if not a stated goal, would be to reduce Social Security to an elderly poverty-reduction program only, eventually possibly even a means-tested one. That would be consistent with the stated World Bank goal of reducing public pillars of retirement programs to financing only elderly poverty prevention. Such a program would require less funding because it would benefit fewer people than the current program. At the same time, cutting and eventually eliminating benefits for the nonpoor would make the working and middle classes more dependent on 401(k)-type private accounts and thereby route more money through the financial services industry.

The Simpson-Bowles report failed to garner the fourteen votes necessary of its eighteen commission members to have it automatically taken up by Congress. Yet, within three weeks of that failure, President Obama agreed to a plan to temporarily reduce Social Security employee payroll taxes from 6.2 to 4.2 percent, the first contribution reduction or tax holiday ever in the history of the program. The purpose was to help stimulate the economy by increasing take-home pay. The shortfall in revenue was made up by other government funds. The danger was that the cut would become permanent if anti-tax sentiment continued, and that, given its shifting politics, Congress could not be relied on to keep making up the shortfall, especially if Social Security would compete with education and other needed programs for scarce funding. Failure to restore the full tax would weaken the stability of the program's financing. It would be a gift to its opponents, who could see it as a self-fulfilling prophecy that the program was not fiscally sustainable.

In early 2013, the full Social Security tax was restored with virtually no public opposition. But at the same time, President Obama announced his support for a proposal to reduce Social Security's COLA as called for by the Simpson-Bowles Commission. Instead of basing the size of each year's benefit rise on the consumer price index, it would be based on a reduced *chained* consumer price index. According to one estimate, the average recipient would lose $16,663 over a thirty-year period.[29] The struggle over Social Security thus has shifted during the past twenty years. Privatization has been off the table since the massive public reaction against former President Bush's 2005 proposal. The goal of Social Security's opponents has shifted to lowering its benefits, first along the comprehensive lines of the Simpson-Bowles Commission proposals and then, when those failed to be adopted, lowering its COLA. In both campaigns to lower its benefits, it was insinuated that Social Security was a cause of the federal government's long-term debt, which in turn was alleged to be undermining the health of the economy. The reality, though, is that Social Security is a separate account that does not contribute to the government's debt, and it holds a surplus.

A more serious but also flawed argument is that Social Security's expenditures *in the long run* will outpace its income and thus must be adjusted downward now to keep the program solvent and not lower future benefits even more. The assumption of a long-term imbalance is a debatable proposition. But even if it were true, there is a far easier and more effective way to address the problem than cutting benefits, which will be discussed in chapter 8: remove the cap on amounts of income as well as on types of income that are subject to Social Security taxation. There is, in short, no fiscally necessary reason to lower Social Security benefits. There are, however, political reasons. Significant elements of the Republican Party are ideologically opposed to Social Security and want to at least trim the size of the program. That makes Social Security reduction a bargaining chip in budget negotiations with Democrats. In addition, as mentioned, the Democratic Party contains its own fifth column of Social Security opponents who are more than willing to cooperate with Republicans on the issue.

Two days after President Obama signed the Social Security tax cut in 2010, the *New York Times* called for long-term cuts in Social Security.[30] That call was an indicator that there is a consensus among even moderately liberal elites that the program be reduced. Elite consensus on reducing the scope of Social Security, though, is not shared by the rest of the country, including the base of the Republican Party. Numerous public opinion polls have demonstrated strong majority support for maintaining or expanding Social Security benefits. In this respect, the clash between elites and the rest of the public reproduces a similar clash over the 1994 NAFTA. It had strong elite support but strong public opposition. Politicians, as always, are caught between what key economic elites and the majority of voters want. Elites have enormous resources, including campaign contributions and lobbyists, at their disposal. Ordinary people are less organized and have only their individual votes. Elites are wealthy enough not to need Social Security benefits for their own retirement. They don't want Social Security to absorb a significant part of the nation's retirement savings because the bulk of their incomes comes from stock market gains. Diverting the retirement investments of ordinary people into stocks increases the values of those stocks and thereby their wealth and income.

TARGETING PUBLIC EMPLOYEES
AND THEIR PENSIONS

Opponents of public employee pensions used the threatened 2013 bankruptcy of Detroit and its municipal employees' pension fund to allege that all public employee pension plans were in serious danger. An article in the *Wall Street Journal*, "Will Your Pension Disappear—Post-Detroit?" commented: "Experts say that now would be a good time for public-sector workers and retirees—especially those whose employers have underfunded pensions—to revisit their retirement plan, crunch out a few what-if scenarios, and adjust their current or planned lifestyle accordingly."[31] A National Public Radio program in the wake of Detroit's bankruptcy announcement used the scare title "Public Pensions under the Gun."[32] An otherwise useful *New York Times* article about actuarial assumptions suggested that Detroit's pension problems were a harbinger for all public pensions.[33]

But the threatened bankruptcy of Detroit's pension plan and resulting reduction of benefits to its retirees are not harbingers for other public pensions. Detroit is an extreme example of a city that lost its industrial tax base, along with much of its population, and is now dealing with a fiscal crisis as a result. The great majority of states and cities with pension plans are nowhere near that situation now or in the foreseeable future. Even with Detroit's very real fiscal problems, there is no necessity to include the pension fund in bankruptcy proceedings. What Detroit does represent is an example of opponents of public employees and their pensions taking advantage of an extraordinary fiscal crisis to further their aims. In that quest, they have developed a successful, disingenuous narrative that public pensions are unsustainable and therefore must be replaced with 401(k) plans, as has been advocated for Detroit.

States, unlike cities, cannot declare bankruptcy, which removes their pension plans from that type of threat. But if right-wing forces have their way, that would change. Politicians like Newt Gingrich and conservative media like the *Weekly Standard* are backing legislation that would allow states to declare bankruptcy.[34] Such a legal declaration would then allow judges to reduce or eliminate pensions. There is, though, not much likelihood that the state bankruptcy campaign will succeed in the near future. State bankruptcy, aside from threatening pension participants, would also threaten the interest of bondholders and stability of financial markets. Both pensioners and bondholders want states to continue to pay their debts and not avoid debt through bankruptcy proceedings.

Given that most private-sector employees lost defined pensions by the 1990s, their continued retention by public employees represents an anomaly to the dominant trend. In the 1980s and early 1990s, that anomaly did not draw much public attention—or ire—because it was thought that pensions were not as good as the shiny new 401(k) plans. But as the first generation to retire under 401(k)s realized—a realization that increasingly spread to other plan members—their retirement incomes were much lower than those of mainly public employees who still had traditional defined benefit pensions. Then the public employee pensions became controversial. Right-wing think tanks such as Cato and Heritage, which were also involved in the campaign against Social Security, fanned opposition to public employee pension plans, building on traditional American anti-tax sentiment and manipulating pension envy into internal class resentment. It was unfair, according to the narrative, that taxpayers had to fund overly generous pensions for undeserving public employees when they themselves only had 401(k)s. A "class war" is looming, according to one columnist, between taxpayers and retired state employees.[35]

The conservative think tanks for the most part, not the financial services industry, are behind the campaign to abolish public employee pensions and replace them with 401(k)s. The relationship between conservative think tanks and the financial services industry is one of convenience rather than direct alignment. The think tanks pursue an ideological goal: attaining as pure a free enterprise capitalist system as possible, while the financial services industry pursues the more tangible goal of maximizing profits. Those goals coincide when think tanks facilitate policy reforms such as Social Security privatization that will enhance prospective profits of the financial services industry. But the priorities of the two are not always the same. The think tanks may want to encourage everyone to provide for their retirement with private accounts as a way of promoting the ideological value of self-reliance, whereas the financial services industry may find servicing only the accounts of relatively prosperous clients to be worthwhile. The think tanks want to increase individual responsibility. They are opposed to defined benefit plans because such plans absolve individuals of risk. Their position thus coincides with that of private employers, the entrepreneurs favored by conservative philosophy. The financial services industry is not concerned with individual responsibility so long as it is able to profit from retirement plans and savings. It can profit from defined benefit plans so long as their contributions are invested in the private market through investment vehicles that it manages.

The conservative think tanks encounter far less public opposition to their campaign against public employee pensions than against Social Security for the simple reason that far fewer people benefit from them. Combined federal, state, and local government workers make up just 14.4 percent of the labor force.[36] On the other hand, public-sector workers have been much more successful in holding on to traditional defined benefit pensions than private-sector workers, largely because they are much more unionized and able to protect themselves. The rate of union membership for public-sector workers (37.4 percent) is over five times that of private-sector workers (7.2 percent).[37]

Like the campaign against Social Security, the campaign against public pensions exaggerates the fiscal problems of the funds. Unlike Social Security, there is no one fund, but many. For the most part, all of the states and municipalities have separate funds. The federal government also has separate funds for its employees. In that scenario of multiple plans, the opponents of public pensions focus on the plans that have the greatest unfunded liabilities and ignore the fully funded ones, presenting the worst cases as typical. Similarly, they focus on the worst cases of participant abuses—public officials who manage to rig up six-figure pensions for themselves at early ages—rather than typical retirees with modest pensions. Another part of the arsenal to win public approval for public-employee pension elimination is to present studies based on prediction models that point to soaring unfunded liabilities. But like all statistical models, a model is only as good as its built-in assumptions. It is easy to rig any model with arbitrary assumptions in order to obtain desired results.

The campaign against public employee pensions reached a fever pitch during the 2008 Great Recession, when the economic slowdown decreased tax revenues and provoked fiscal crises at state and local levels. Those crises produced opportunities to shift the blame from the recession to public employee pensions. Those pension systems must be ended, it was advocated, and replaced by 401(k)s in order to restore balance to public budgets and avoid future tax increases. In state legislature after state legislature, the corporate-funded conservative American Legislative Exchange Council (ALEC) facilitated the introduction of bills to replace employee pension systems with 401(k)-type plans. In a 2013 report titled, "Keeping the Promise: State Solutions for Government Pension Reform," it reiterated its position that "legislators should move from defined-benefit systems to properly designed alternatives, such as defined-contribution, cash-balance, or hybrid plans."[38] The campaign to replace pensions with 401(k) plans for new employees has succeeded in many cities and, at the state level, in Alaska, with bills pending in nearly all other legislatures.

Despite the success of right-wing think tanks in forming a public perception of public pensions as costly, unsustainable, and unfair, there is a stubborn reality that they are less costly than 401(k)s, sustainable, and fair, if you think that all workers deserve adequate retirement income. In a careful study sponsored by the National Institute on Retirement Security, economist Beth Almeida and actuary William B. Fornia concluded that "the cost to deliver the same level of retirement income to a group of employees is 46% lower in a defined benefit plan [whether public or private] than it is in a defined contribution plan."[39] Put differently, if a public entity sets the delivery of a certain amount of replacement income as a goal for its retirement plan, it will be less costly to do that with a defined benefit plan than a 401(k) or other defined contribution plan. Switching to a 401(k) plan would be more—not less—expensive. It would only be less expensive if the employer did not care about maintaining employee income in retirement and contributed less to the 401(k).

The Almeida and Fornia study assumes that the contributions are actually made. Public as well as private pension funds have often run into trouble precisely because contributions weren't made. States and cities have forgone contributions in order to balance budgets during revenue shortfalls. New Jersey Republican Governor Chris Christie in 2011, for example, refused to make a required state contribution of $3.1 billion. These types of pension payment holidays during fiscal crises would be acceptable if they were considered as loans by public employees that needed to be paid back during better times. Indeed, public employees could then be seen as heroes who were bailing out state budgets during bad times. Instead they are fodder for self-fulfilling prophecies that traditional pensions are unsustainable. No long-term pension or retirement savings plan is sustainable if necessary contributions are not made to it.

Employer failure to adequately contribute to pension funds is the leading cause of unfunded liabilities. Some public pension funds are fully funded, others overfunded—yes, *over*funded—and others underfunded, the ones that selectively receive all the press attention and ire. A Boston College Center for Retirement Research study of 126 public pension plans found that the average plan was overfunded at 102 percent in 2001. That year's recession lowered balances. In 2008, at the depth of the Great Recession, the average plan was funded at 84 percent, still above the 80 percent that experts believe to be the goal. As of 2011, the average balance was at 75 percent.[40] I'm still waiting to see an article about the many public pension funds that are in very good shape despite the recession. The only recent article I've seen about overfunding was about a private pension fund. When Amazon's Jeff Bezos bought the *Washington Post* in 2013, it was revealed that the employee pension fund was significantly overfunded at 141 percent due to bountiful investment returns.[41]

As a result of the recession, nearly all public pensions have some amount of unfunded liabilities, as in Detroit. They can exist with liabilities and not endanger their ability to make payments because they partially operate, like Social Security, on pay-as-you-go principles. Active workers pay contributions as money is paid out to pensioners. Putting a hard stop to any pension fund, as bankruptcy would do, would starve it of new contributions, setting up an eventual unnecessary inability to make payments.

Public as well as private pension funds can have unfunded liabilities because their benefits are guaranteed. To make good on those guarantees, plan sponsors must ensure that the plans are properly funded. Because 401(k)s have no guaranteed benefits, by definition they have no liabilities, funded or unfunded. Their sponsors are thus completely absolved of any responsibility for proper funding. If a state skips payments to a public pension fund as a means of making up for revenue shortfalls during recessions, that will come back to haunt it in the form of an increased unfunded liability that must be addressed when the economy improves. If an employer skips payments to a 401(k), it can do so without fear of having to face any future reckoning. All future consequences will be borne by workers at retirement.

CHAPTER 5

How 401(k)s Are Supposed to Work and Why They Don't

The conversion to 401(k) and other defined contribution (DC) plans, along with the growth of Individual Retirement Accounts (IRAs), over the past three decades has been a boon for the private retirement business in the United States. As of 2013, according to the Investment Company Institute, $11.1 trillion was held in these private accounts, double the $5.5 trillion held in 2000. Over the same period, the 401(k) portion of private accounts grew from $1.7 trillion to $3.8 trillion. Public and private defined benefit (DB) pension plans held $7.9 trillion, 41.8 percent of total retirement plan assets. That was down from the 48.1 percent proportion held in 2000, reflecting their decreasing availability as options for employees.[1] All private and DB accounts involve stock market investing. Thus, the financial services industry derives profits from DB plans as well as private accounts, though not as much. The other major actor in retirement provision, Social Security, is outside the stock market; its funds are held in government bonds.

Since 1970, the financial services industry has increased from 2.9 to 5.9 percent of the gross domestic product, from 3.7 to 4.2 percent of all corporate employees, and from accounting for 19.1 to 27.1 percent of all corporate profits. Driving that increase were the introduction of IRAs in 1975 and the takeoff of 401(k)s in 1981.[2] As significant as the growth of the financial part of the economy, even more attention grabbing is that, with only 4.2 percent of all employees, the financial services industry captures a whopping 27.1 percent of profits.

The federal government subsidizes the financial services industry with tax exemptions for retirement contributions. In 2011, the value of tax exemptions for IRA, 401(k), and other retirement plans was $111.7 billion. Together with the value of the mortgage interest deduction for home ownership, it represented 20.4 percent of the total $1.06 trillion budget that includes forgone income from exemptions as well as actual funds expended.[3] From a taxpayer's perspective, deductions for retirement contributions and interest payments on mortgages are welcome reliefs. From the perspective of the financial services industry, they are enticements for consumers to part with more of their income.

The massive conversion to 401(k) and other defined contribution plans was responsible for driving much of the industry's profit expansion over the past three decades. At the same time, though, retirement security has decreased because these plans do not support retirees nearly as much as the defined benefit plans that they replaced. To see why, we have to examine how the plans are supposed to function and what they actually produce.

What all defined contribution plans, of which the 401(k) is a variation, along with IRAs have in common is that participants invest money in the stock market and then use the accumulated values of those investments to finance their retirement. There are no guarantees in this system. It's all based on how much people individually accumulate, with the people bearing all investment risks.

There are two phases of defined contribution accounts: *accumulation* while actively working and *spending down* afterward to provide retirement income. Participants accumulate while they work and put money into their accounts. They spend down after they retire. The accumulation phase is clear to most people because, as with bank accounts, they see their money going in and they get periodic statements that (hopefully) show their growing balances. But most people have little idea what is supposed to happen when they actually do retire, something we will explore presently. Both phases are plagued with problems that make it nearly impossible for participants to achieve adequate retirement security.

HOW MUCH DO YOU NEED TO RETIRE?

Most people have no idea how much they need to accumulate to adequately finance their retirement. They see their savings going up year by year for the most part. They will soon have much more money in their retirement account than in their checking and savings accounts, and eventually more money than their houses are worth. It seems like a great deal of money. However, what most people do not know is how far this money will go in terms of financing retirement.

To understand this, we have to look first at what is called technically *income replacement*: the percentage of final salary that the plan replaces in retirement. For example, if you retire when your final salary has reached $50,000 and your plan gives you $40,000 to live on in retirement, that would mean that you had an income replacement of 40,000 divided by 50,000, which equals an 80 percent rate.

For people to maintain their standard of living in retirement, they need to have an income flow that is as close as possible to what they had during their final working years. In some cases, they will have lower expenses and not need as much income. Children are likely to be grown and on their own. Houses are likely to be paid off. They will no longer have to save for retirement. But in other cases, they will likely have more expenses, as medical costs increase when people age.

There is no consensus among retirement experts about exactly how much of final income needs to be replaced. The most conservative estimate I have seen is 50 percent. Most, however, place it much higher. In a survey of financial planners, Flora L. Williams and Helen Zhou found that recommendations ranged between 75 percent and 90 percent.[4] An Urban Institute report put the target at 80 percent.[5] Some retirement experts, such as economist Teresa Ghilarducci, argue that people need 100 percent.[6] There are a lucky few, difficult as that may be to imagine, whose retirement plans do provide that much income.

Sometimes, that income replacement comes from one source, a single retirement plan from a single employer. Most people, though, draw retirement income from several sources. The classic three-legged stool is to have retirement income from Social Security, an employment defined benefit pension plan, and personal savings. Many retirement income situations are still more complicated, with separate incomes from different employers during their careers. Personal retirement savings may have different parts. Some may have invested money in real estate and use its returns during retirement. They may also have inherited wealth that will provide retirement income. Technically, inheritances are not savings since they were not *saved* from normal working incomes. Inherited wealth and retirement savings can also become linked, as when an inherited house frees up money that would otherwise be spent on mortgage payments so that it can be invested in an IRA instead. The key figure is how much all of the different retirement income streams add up to in terms of income replacement.

People who still have traditional DB pensions are much more likely to think in terms of income replacement than people with only DC plans. They will say things like, "I will retire when I reach 80 percent." People who have DC plans are more likely to think in terms of how large their portfolios are. They think of how much they have accumulated and then have a very vague notion of how that will support them in retirement. A large part of this is because DC plans, unlike DB ones, contain no guarantees about how much income will be replaced.

For defined contribution plans, the question is: how much accumulation is needed to replace at least 70 percent of retirement income? The answer depends on *how* the spend-down phase will be conducted. There are three options: lump-sum withdrawal, active management, and annuitization. Participants can withdraw their accumulations as lump sums and use them as they like. They could take the money, with severe tax consequences, and purchase, say, a Greek island on which to live out their retirement years, assuming that they had built up enough. The problem with that is that they would have the island but no income to support themselves.

The more prudent course of action would be to manage the accumulation they built up, their personal capital, in such a way that they can live off it. That's the option of active management. They're in some control, but they are still at the mercy of the stock market. The level at which they will be able to finance their living expenses will depend on how well their investments perform. The most common strategy is to systematically withdraw funds from the nest egg during retirement at a rate that ensures that it will last for the rest of their lives.

Active management requires a choice of goals: to preserve an estate for heirs or to maximize income to support retirement. If the first, then the strategy is to withdraw in such a way that the principal accumulation is preserved and to live off its dividend, interest, and capital gains. The principal remains throughout the retirement years until death, when it passes to heirs. What is gained in terms of having personal wealth to leave to heirs is at the expense of income during retirement. Withdrawal rates would vary according to stock market gains and losses.

The second active management strategy involves a higher rate of withdrawals from the accumulation such that it includes a part of the principal as well. For this scenario, until recently there had been considerable agreement that up to 4.5 percent could be withdrawn without danger of outliving the money (principal and gains). This yields a higher income, but results in less or nothing that is inheritable. The 4.5 percent withdrawal strategy came to be known among financial planners as simply the "4 percent rule." It was based on a 1993 study by financial planner Bill Bengen that concluded that if retirees withdrew 4.5 percent each year for their living expenses from a portfolio with a 60–40 split between stocks and bonds, the money would last at least thirty years before being depleted. A retiree, for example, with a 401(k) accumulation of $100,000, could start out withdrawing $4,500 for the first year of retirement, and then 4.5 percent of the remaining balance each subsequent year. That, though, assumed average earnings of 8 percent on the portfolio, an assumption that has been thrown into great doubt since the 2008 Great Recession. As a result, the 4 percent rule is, as a *New York Times* headline put it, "golden no more," with planners now recommending lower rates of withdrawal.[7] There are two fundamental problems, though, with this strategy, whatever the rate: the rate of withdrawal allowed is very low—a $1 million accumulation would only yield $45,000 annually, and even with that low withdrawal rate, if you live more than thirty years, you could run out of money.

The third option of annuitizing increases the retirement income somewhat and eliminates the risk of outliving the money. Annuities are products sold mostly by life insurance companies. Purchasers give the company some of their accumulations, say, $100,000. In return, the company guarantees that it will pay them a percentage of that for a certain time. While there are multiple types of annuities, what we are interested in are life annuities. They produce a result most like having a traditional defined benefit pension: a guaranteed income for life after retirement, however short or long that turns out to be. It is the option that we will analyze for comparison purposes with traditional DB pensions.

Annuities are commonly considered pensions. I think this is a misnomer. Annuities are not pensions. A pension is the product of a defined benefit plan. An annuity is what someone could receive or purchase as a result of accumulations in a DC plan. I therefore speak of pensions only in relation to DB plans and speak of annuities in relationship to DC plans. Put more plainly, if you are in a DB plan, you will receive a pension. If you are in a DC plan, you may receive an annuity if you so choose.

A life insurance company that issues annuities is a cross between a bank and a casino. It takes your money and returns it to you on a gamble that you will die before it has to pay you more than it has taken from you. In the case of annuities, the insurance company is betting that the purchaser—the annuitant—will die before it has to pay out an amount of money greater than the purchase cost plus what it could make from investing that amount. In order to make sure that they win as many bets as possible, insurance companies employ actuaries who are mathematical specialists in calculating and pricing statistical risks. The risk of a seventy-year-old living twenty years longer, for example, is less than the risk of a sixty-year-old living that much longer. That allows the company to sell an annuity to the older purchaser for a lower price. Essentially, actuaries calculate longevities and probabilities of death and then translate those calculations into prices and profit probabilities for life insurance companies.

The amount of an annuity that can be afforded depends on the size of the accumulated portfolio at the time of retirement. That size in turn depends in part on the timing of the retirement, given the ups and downs of the stock market. Someone who retired in early 2006 would have been in better shape than someone who retired in late 2008, just after the market crash.

Now that we've considered the spend-down possibilities, we're back to the question of how much you need to accumulate in a 401(k) or other defined contribution plan to finance retirement. The quick but rough answer, depending on the source, is eight to eleven times your final salary if there will also be full Social Security benefits.[8] Without Social Security benefits, sixteen to twenty-two times the final salary is needed.

A more precise estimation based on the annuitizing option is provided in table 5.1. The first column lists various final incomes. The closer you are to retirement, the easier this will be to estimate. The second column, retirement income needed, is the total income needed from all sources in order to reach a minimum 70 percent wage replacement. It is based on the assumption that there are no other sources of retirement income. It is an annuity that includes a cost-of-living adjustment (COLA) increase to keep up with inflation.

If you are like most Americans and will have Social Security benefits, you will not need as much as is indicated by the last two columns. You will need to calculate how much additional income you need after taking into account what you will receive from Social Security. To do that, look at your estimated benefits on the Social Security statement that you receive once a year. You can also get an online estimate from Social Security. Your benefit is presented as a monthly payment. Multiply that by 12 and then subtract the total from your retirement income

TABLE 5.1

Annuity Cost to Replace 70 Percent of Final Salary with Cost-of-Living Adjustment at Age 65

Final Salary	Retirement Income Needed	Annuity Cost*	
		Men	Women
$30,000	$21,000	$403,846	$446,809
$50,000	$35,000	$673,077	$744,681
$75,000	$52,500	$1,009,615	$1,117,021
$100,000	$70,000	$1,346,154	$1,489,362
$150,000	$105,000	$2,019,231	$2,234,043

*At 5.2 percent and 4.7 percent payout rates for men and women, respectively (rates vary).

Source: Calculated by the author.

needed. Multiply that by 0.7 to get the income needed to be replaced by your 401(k) or other defined contribution accumulation. If you multiply that by 100 and then divide the result by 5.2 if you are a man and 4.7 if you are a woman, you will have the accumulation amount that you will need.

When I went through this exercise at age sixty-five, I found that despite thirty years of relatively generous contributions from my employer and me plus substantial extra contributions and Social Security—a whopping 41.4 percent of my income altogether—I would only be able to replace about 48 percent of my income if I retired.[9] At that rate, I would be able to retire in another thirty years at age ninety-five! But maybe not. That would assume that my income was the same in thirty years. If I was able to stay employed and received raises, even minimal COLAs, in my doddering old age, I would have to accumulate even more. It would be like being told to swim out to a boat sailing away nearly as fast as you were swimming. You're making progress, and maybe with several lifetimes you might get there.

I did not always save 41.4 percent of my income for retirement. It varied from that amount to a minimum of my retirement plan plus

Social Security, which was 25.4 percent of income when mortgage and education payments for my children took precedence. But that minimum was still more than most working people are able to put away. If the system should have worked for anyone, it should have been me with the advantages that I had.

I suspect that if you go through the exercise of calculating how much you need to accumulate, you will come to the same sobering conclusion that I did: that it is impossible during any kind of normal or even extended work career to accumulate enough. You might be able to improve your odds of getting closer to the goal, but you are very unlikely to reach the 70 percent goal in the best of circumstances. To understand why, we have to look at the ways in which the accumulation and spend-down phases are loaded against participants.

WHY PARTICIPANTS CAN'T ACCUMULATE ENOUGH

The major problem is obvious: not enough money is saved to achieve a large enough accumulation to finance adequate replacement income. While the financial services industry uses this fact to call on DC participants to increase their rates of saving, the more fundamental question, as alluded to already, is whether it would be possible for anyone, no matter how frugal their spending habits, to put away enough money in these accounts. To get an approximation of what it would take to achieve an 80 percent preretirement income replacement rate combined from Social Security and a DC account at age sixty-six, an Urban Institute report based on modeling market outcomes estimated that a single, low-income worker would have to start saving 16 percent of income in the accounts, starting at age twenty-five. The higher the income and the later the start date for saving, the greater the percentage of income needed to save. A single high earner starting at age forty-five would have to put 45 percent of income in a DC account.[10] Average contribution rates are far less than what the Urban Institute model indicates are necessary. An Employee Benefits Research Institute study found that employees contributed an average 7.5 percent of salary to DC plans, while a Plan Council of America study found that employers contributed an average of only 2.5 percent.[11] The combined 10 percent is far less than the 16 percent needed for a single worker starting at age twenty-five, the category that needs the least in the Urban Institute model.

Whatever the amount that ends up in these accounts, their growth will be severely compromised by management fees, commissions, and profits. Defined contribution participants typically lose from 20 to 30 percent and more of their accumulations to investment management fees charged by the financial services industry. Without those losses, a $300,000 accumulation would have been $360,000 or greater, which in turn would have translated into a correspondingly higher annuity payout upon retirement. According to a Demos study, the typical American household will pay $155,000 in 401(k) fees, losing 30.3 percent of their potential accumulation to them.[12] The administrative overhead costs for defined benefit plans are much lower, though, surprisingly, there are no national comparative studies.[13] A part, but only a part, of the reason why DC plans have more administrative costs is because it takes more time to manage fifty individual DC personal plans than it does to manage one common DB plan. Beyond that honest difference, the financial services industry has multiple opportunities to charge fees and commissions for its services to DC plan participants. Most of these fees are hidden. By law, DC plan participants must receive regular statements with information about their accounts. That doesn't mean, though, that the statements must disclose what fees have been taken out. Nor does it mean that the statements have to present their information clearly.

The 401(k) and other DC plan balance statements vary in how much information they disclose about fees and commissions. Some disclose only account balances. Others include information on expenses, but it is deceptively limited information. The most accessible fee is that charged by the administrator of the plan, sometimes called the third-party administrator fee. That company will charge a percentage of the account balance, but since the administrator is putting your money into other funds, the administrative charges don't stop there. Each of those funds has its own administrative fees. To determine that, you have to find the "expense ratio" of the fund.

Deloitte Consulting LLP surveyed 130 defined contribution plans in terms of what it called "all-in" fees, which combined the third-party administrator and expense ratio fees. It found a range between 0.35 and 2.37 with a median of 0.72. In general, the greater the assets and number of participants in a plan, the lower the likely fee. Plans with fewer than one hundred participants paid an average of 2.03 percent of assets in fees compared to 0.49 percent for plans with ten thousand or more participants.[14]

That may be just the tip of an iceberg in which there are greater, more deeply hidden fees. If I invest in a fund that is made up of other funds, a fund of funds, each of the combined funds will have separate fees that are not reflected in the fees of the parent fund. Commissions that are paid by mutual funds to brokers for purchases and sales are not included in expense ratios and are thus also hidden. There are multiple other hidden rake-offs to which you could be subject, which have such financial services industry names as wrap fees, mortality and expense charges, surrender charges, money market spreads, and floats.[15] Then, not to be forgotten, wherever your investment ultimately lands, you will not receive all of the profits that it facilitates. The company where the investment is made will deduct its expenses, which could include large CEO bonuses, before distributing dividends to shareholders. By treating bonuses as expenses rather than profits, top managers essentially use an accounting trick to expropriate profits for their own use rather than distributing them to owners, including 401(k) investors. It is a practice that is all the easier when the 401(k) "owners" are so far removed from any actual control over what they theoretically own.

When the fees, commissions, and profits are added up, their impact is far greater on accumulations than the sum would indicate. The US Securities and Exchange Commission (SEC) has shown that even a mere 1 percent increase from 0.5 percent to 1.5 percent in fees deducted over twenty years for a $10,000 investment with a 10 percent average return would reduce the final balance by 17 percent from $60,000 to $49,725.[16] For lower average growth rates, proportionate losses to the fees will be still greater. When stock market growth rates are low or flat, the impact of 401(k) and other defined contribution plan fees, commissions, and profits grows.

You might take the attitude that the fees and other drainages are an irksome annoyance, but at least with many 401(k) plans, you are in control of investing decisions and can manage your portfolio. But is that a good idea? It might be if you know what you are doing and want to spend your time researching and making those decisions. But most people have neither the knowledge nor the inclination to skillfully control their portfolios. Economists Alicia H. Munnell and Annika Sundén argue that when it comes to investing decisions, most 401(k) participants are rank amateurs who often make classic mistakes.[17] As in gambling, flooding the game with amateurs works to the advantage of professionals. To know what you are doing in investing requires an understanding of the principles of investing, which few people have. Even if you understand those principles, you still need further information about the stocks you are interested in buying and selling. Unless you think you can get that information from hunches or tips, you will not be on even ground with professional investors who have very expensive research resources at their disposal, often provided with the aid of sophisticated software and massive computer power. You will be in a game that is loaded against you in favor of the professionals.

You might be able to partially mitigate this disadvantage by hiring a personal financial adviser, an occupation that has grown enormously with the growth of 401(k) plans and is part of the financial services industry. Personal financial advisers as a distinct occupational category first made an appearance in the *Statistical Abstract of the United States* for the year 2003, which found some 315,000 or 0.228 percent of the nation's labor force. By 2010, their ranks had increased to 369,000 or 0.265 percent of the labor force.[18] By paying such a specialist, of course, you would be parting with still more of your money, though it might make sense if it keeps you from making bad investment choices.

Like gambling advice, though, investing advice is hardly an exact science. You could be paying money for advice that turns out to be bad or in the interest of the adviser rather than you. Many advisers earn significant commissions by selling financial products to clients to whom they do not have legally binding fiduciary responsibilities. Whether to engage a personal financial adviser to guide retirement accumulation decisions is not an issue for members of defined benefit plans. Their employers hire professionals to make pension investment decisions.

The investment performances of DB plans are superior to DC ones precisely because they are directed by professionals. According to Munnell and Sundén's calculations, between 1985 and 2001, DB plans had an average 7.9 percent rate of return, compared to 7.1 percent for DC plans, outperforming them by 11 percent.[19] Consulting firm Towers Watson found that DB plans outperformed DC plans between 1995 and 2011 by an average 8.01 percent to 7.25 percent growth rate. DC plans outperformed DB plans only during a few boom stock market years.[20]

Even if you know (or are lucky) enough to invest well, you still face another problem for the growth of your accumulation. In theory, participants in DC plans and their employers steadily make contributions over the working career. The system is built on an assumption that contributions will be made that will have a long time to gain value. The longer the contributions stay in the fund to gather interest and capital gains, the greater the overall accumulation. If a thousand dollars is left for thirty years at an average 7 percent gain, it will be worth an impressive $7,612, or over seven-and-a-half times the original amount. That sounds great, but the reality is that for most workers, their early contributions are very low because their salaries are low at the beginning of their careers. The advantages of capital gains and compounding interest are offset by the low initial amounts invested. A colleague wishes that he had been able to save a million dollars in one of these accounts during his twenties. He thinks he would have then been set for life. When I asked him how that would have been possible, he was at a loss to answer, except to say that he would have delayed starting a family.

Another assumption of the system is that people will steadily make contributions. The reality is that most workers can't make steady contributions because they change jobs during their careers. Some of the positions may be covered by 401(k) plans and others not. During downturns, employers may also suspend contributions. The consistency of contributions will thus vary. Every missed contribution will cost the overall accumulation that amount plus all that it would have increased in capital gains or interest. A missed $10,000 of contributions, following the SEC example above, would twenty years later amount to a loss of $49,725.

To aggravate the problem of not enough money going into the plans, sizable amounts are "leaked" each year as a result of cash-outs and unrepaid loans. In a comprehensive study, Matt Fellows and Katy Willemin found that in 2010, $70 billion was withdrawn from DC plans.[21] To put that in perspective, as employers and employees were contributing $293 billion to the plans, employees were withdrawing $70 billion from them. Of the $70 billion withdrawn, only $10 billion was in the form of loans that would be repaid. The $60 billion bulk leaves the system permanently for nonretirement expenses. Low-income participants are more likely than higher-income groups to cash out when they leave or lose jobs. For them, 401(k) accounts are often their only savings. Such cash-outs have become a form of severance pay. According to Social Security Administration–funded research, at any given time, about 20 percent of the participants in those plans have outstanding loans.[22] When participants get into financial tight spots through loss of jobs, children's educational expenses, medical bills, or just plain irresponsible spending habits, they are tempted and able to raid their accumulations. Some companies have evolved 401(k) and IRA debit cards, though these have provoked heavy criticism and proposed legislation by US senators Herb Kohl and Michael Enzi to ban them.

In technical terms, substantial parts of DC plan funds, unlike DB funds, are alienable, which means that they can be used for purposes other than their original intent—to finance retirement. The obvious problem is that the more that is taken out of retirement accounts, the less there is to finance retirement. It is usually easier to spend than pay back borrowed money. When the lender is a bank or other powerful institution, it has legal and other resources to make sure that it is paid back. It is quite another matter when the borrower and lender are one and the same, as when people borrow from their 401(k) accounts. They face few immediate negative consequences for not paying back. At worst, if they are under age fifty-nine and a half, there is a 10 percent tax penalty on the amount they do not pay back. The more serious consequences are in the future, the further they are away from retirement. That makes it all the more tempting and easier to raid their accounts. It is like using money in a pinch from a savings account.

In addition to the problems of contributing to these accounts and the losses sustained from management fees and other drainages, and any leakages from withdrawals, participants face stock market volatility. Unlike DB plan participants who have predictable incomes, DC plan participants must worry about the timing of stock market ups and downs. They are caught in a dilemma. They can invest conservatively in bonds and be assured of steady but low yields or they can invest in equities (stocks) and have higher long-term yields but with more volatile ups and downs. The traditional advice was to invest in stocks early in a career, leave them for the long term, and then near retirement shift to bonds to avoid short-term plunges in values that could delay retirement.

People about to retire when the 2008 Great Recession hit who were holding substantial parts of their portfolios in equities had no choice but to delay retirement. The market plunged from a high of 14,034 in 2007 to a low of 6,594 in 2009, a drop of 53 percent. According to an Economic Benefit Research Institute study, the average 401(k) plan with over $200,000 lost a quarter of its value.[23] It took four years until 2013 for the market to recover its previous high. At that, stocks were getting back to their values of nearly six years earlier in 2007. More important than the money lost was the time lost in being able to accumulate enough to retire. Each 401(k) participant's situation was different, depending on the type and mix of investments. But even those whose losses were less than the average went through enormous anxiety because there was no guarantee that the market would ever rebound. All had to decide whether to keep working, if that was an option, or live on less retirement income than planned—a choice that no one should have to make. It is one thing to have to make such a forced choice when you are healthy and able to keep working and quite another when you are in your sixties or seventies.

Much of the culture around investing takes as an article of faith that in the long run the market will always grow. Smart investors should be in it for the long term and not be rattled by short-term dips, according to such popular business authors as finance professor Jeremy J. Siegel, whose popular *Stocks for the Long Run* went through four editions from 1994 to 2007, curiously just before the Great Recession began. But *Business Week* writers William Wolman and Anne Colamosca, in their 2002 book, *The Great 401(k) Hoax*, were not so sure. Using information about stock market performance that went back to the early 1800s, they detected a pattern in which the market reached peaks based on artificially overinflated prices that were followed by crashes that then took several decades to recover from. Short-run performance is thus always a very risky predictor of long-run performance. The authors argued that the year 2000 represented such a peak, and returns would be flat for at least a decade after.[24]

After the 1929 crash, the market took twenty-six years to fully recover. In 1966, the market reached an artificial high of 985 and then fell, taking until 1983, seventeen years, to fully recover. In 2001, the market reached 11,337. Ten years later, the market was below that level for most of 2011. Throughout these long-term rises and falls, there have been shorter rises and falls. Following the peak of 11,337 in 2001, the market built up to 14,034 in 2007 but then spectacularly fell again. Participants in 401(k)s were on a roller coaster during the decade, with some drops more heart stopping than others. What made the lost values seem like less was that they were partially offset by new contributions. If the value of a portfolio fell by 10 percent but, at the same time, the participant made new contributions that were worth 5 percent of the portfolio, then it *seemed* like there was only a drop of 5 percent. At the same time, the financial services industry, as always, kept urging participants to increase their contributions, as if they were responsible for making up for what was being lost in the market.

The initial optimism over what 401(k)s and similar defined contribution plans could deliver came at a time—the early 1980s through the late 1990s—when the market seemed to be on an ever upward course. It was easy to convince people that if present market trends continued (famous last words), all would bode well. It would have been much more difficult to win public acceptance of 401(k)s if they had been launched for the first time during the last ten years. That's why the argument that is used to promote them has shifted from "they are the best form of retirement plan" to "they are the only affordable form for private and public-sector employers."

In sum, a host of factors—low contributions, high management fees, gaps in coverage, lack of professional investing, and so on—afflict and compromise the ability of defined contribution plans to build up sufficient accumulations to adequately finance retirement incomes. What solution does the financial services industry offer? It uses massive well-financed advertising campaigns bordering on moral crusades to urge workers to save more for retirement than their plans require. The hidden and open messages are that those who diligently save will be amply rewarded in their golden years, while those who don't will suffer the consequences.

The *CTDCP News*, a newsletter that ING sent out to participants in the DC plan I was enrolled in, used a four-color chart to demonstrate that if a twenty-five-year-old worker started out by saving $200 per pay period and maintained that for forty years until retirement at sixty-five, there would be an accumulation of $827,742, assuming a 6 percent rate of return.[25] This seemed impressive, since $827,742 would be sufficient to purchase annual annuities with COLAs of $40,455 for women and $43,042 for men at current rates—more than enough to maintain the preretirement incomes of average workers, which were $40,712 at the time of the newsletter.

It was, though, an argument built on half-truths, missing information, and deceptions. ING admitted without elaboration that "taxes and any applicable product-related charges are not reflected." Taxes would be a substantial problem, as we will see shortly, and "product-related charges" certainly would be because they would reduce the overall accumulation by a minimal 20 percent.

By far, though, the biggest problem was in a deceptive sleight of hand that ING employed. Saving $200 a pay period to obtain $827,742 over forty years appeared reasonable since it is 13 percent of the average worker's current income, according to national income data. But the hypothetical diligent saver would have had to begin forty years ago when the average annual income was just $6,200.[26] To have begun the $200 savings plan then, he or she would have had to put aside a whopping 80 percent of pay—an impossibility for all but the independently wealthy. Even if that worker could somehow have done that, the amount would have exceeded the limits permitted by tax-sheltered retirement plans.

It is impossible to know what the average wage will be forty years from now and how much would have to be saved to afford a requisite retirement annuity. For sure, with inflation the required annuity purchase price to adequately replace the income of an average wage worker will be a lot higher than $827,742. Those who start the $200 saving plan that ING advocates will find themselves on a slippery slope on which, as their accumulations nominally grow, they will be worth less in retirement security. Forty years from now, $827,742 will not look as impressive as it does today.

The advice of ING and the other financial services industry corporations in the savings moral crusade turns out to be much more self-serving than a feasible prescription for building retirement security. The more extra savings that workers put into the plans, the more that the financial services industry collects in administrative fees, commissions, and other charges. Putting extra savings in the plans may help to top off other streams of retirement income, especially if workers are eligible for adequate defined benefit pensions, but it is not a strategy that can be relied on alone to bolster the much lower 401(k) incomes enough to provide adequate retirement security.

BAD OPTIONS FOR RETIREE SAVINGS

The 401(k) and other defined contribution plans do not just have an accumulation problem. The financial services industry also controls and takes more pounds of flesh during the spend-down phase. As we have seen, aside from lump-sum withdrawal, which is generally not prudent, retirees with DC account accumulations have two options for using those funds to finance their retirements: active management and annuitizing. With both options, the financial services industry continues to extract profits, as it does during the accumulation phase, getting participants coming and going.

If you choose the option of active management, depending on how you do it, you could continue to be subject to management fees. You could, for example, leave the money with the 401(k) or other DC plan administrator as you gradually spent it down, continuing as before to choose places to invest it. In all cases, you would be subject to the same embedded hidden fees, commissions, and profit taking that you were during the accumulation phase.

No form of active management has the advantage of risk pooling. In order to ensure that you don't run out of money, you can withdraw only a small amount. As a result, if you survive relatively few years in retirement, you will have had to live on less income than you could have. The money left in your account will be good news for your heirs but at the expense of your own retirement standard of living. If you last well into your nineties, to make your money last that long you can have only a low rate of withdrawal in order to avoid living longer than your money.

The superiority of defined benefit pensions is that their withdrawal rates are based on pooled longevity estimates. For example, based on Social Security actuarial tables, a sixty-five-year-old male retiree can be expected to live eighteen more years to eighty-three and a female twenty years to eighty-five.[27] That means that a sixty-five-year-old retiree can have an income assumed to last just eighteen or twenty years, depending on gender—an eighteen- or twenty-year spend-down rather than the thirty years that financial planners recommend for active management. Those who live longer—to ninety, for example—will have income that is based on a nineteen-year spend-down, since by law, DB plans must use blended gender longevity assumptions. An income that is based on a nineteen-year spend-down will inevitably be more than one based on the actual twenty-five-year spend-down of those living to ninety. What makes this possible for defined benefit pensions—but not actively managed funds—is that other members of the pool will die before ages eighty-three or eighty-five. Their money will remain in the pool to continue funding those who live longer than average. The short-lived subsidize the long lived.

Annuitizing of DC accounts gains only *some* of the advantages in increased income possibilities of risk pooling of DB plans because it is on the less-favorable for-profit terms of the financial services industry. Annuitizing also comes at the expense of losing ownership of the wealth and the possibility of leaving it to heirs. By using the advantages of pooling, insurance companies are able to offer annuities with spend-down rates that are at least 30 percent higher than the less than 4 percent withdrawal rate now recommended for active management.

Affecting the size of annuity income is the interest rate of the annuity itself. Here, there is a distinction. There is the interest rate that is based on how much can be made from the money. For example, if $100,000 is invested in a bond and the bond pays 2 percent, then there is that 2 percent interest. But we are not looking at that. We are looking at what is called the *payout* rate. The payout rate is the percentage of the principal or purchase price that the insurance company promises to pay for the life of the annuity.

To understand how payout rates work, first compare them with the interest that you receive for a savings account. If you have $10,000 in a savings account, the bank will give you a rate of interest for it, say 2 percent. At the end of one year, your balance will grow to $10,200 and you are free to withdraw that amount of money in order to, say, buy a car. Obviously, the bank hasn't just given you the extra $200 out of the goodness of its heart. During that year, it has invested the $10,000 and received a higher rate of interest than what it is paying you to use your money. A bank is in business to make, not give, money. You gain and the bank gains. You have allowed the bank to invest your personal capital, and in return, it has taken part of the gain on your capital for itself.

When you purchase an annuity, as with a savings account, the company invests the money and shares the proceeds with you. But unlike a savings account, you no longer own the money; the company does. This is bad news for your heirs but good news for you because it allows for greater retirement income. In addition to the interest payments, the company adds a second sum based on returning the original cost of the annuity to you—the principal—gradually over the length of the annuity. This is called the amortization rate. It is as if you had loaned the company the amount of the annuity purchase price and it is paying you back the principal plus interest. Because annuity payout rates combine both interest and amortization rates, they are inevitably higher than interest rates alone.

Payout rates for annuities between 2000 and 2010 varied, but not nearly as much as interest rates. They've varied less because they are primarily based not on the interest that the company can make from the money but rather on the likely longevity of the annuitant. Market interest rates change much more dramatically than actuarial estimations of how long people are likely to survive. Payout rates go up and down, and it would be to anyone's advantage to purchase an annuity when it is at a high point. But the difference between the high and low points over the ten years from 2000 and 2010 is a difference of less than 1 percent. Between 2000 and 2010, payout rates for a single life annuity, which did not include a COLA, varied between highs of 9.1 percent and 8.3 percent to lows of 7.6 percent and 7.1 percent for men and women, respectively. Those are important differences, but they're not as great a difference as occurred between general interest rates during that same period of time, which varied between 3.25 and 9.5 percent.

Despite being less volatile than interest rates, annuity payout rates have in fact fallen dramatically since 401(k) plans were initiated in the early 1980s. They have fallen less than interest rates but neverthe-less have dropped significantly. In 1986, a life annuity purchased for $100,000 yielded a monthly retirement income of $977 for men and $931 for women. In 2010, an annuity for that same cost yielded only $631 for men and $531 for women—35 percent less.[28] High annuity payout rates in the early 1980s reflected the inflationary 1970s. As in-flation came down, so did payout rates, continuing to this day.

Sellers of annuities make sure that they will receive a profit by set-ting the payout rate for a longer longevity than your actual one. It is like a casino that sets the payout rate for winning at roulette lower than the actual odds of winning to ensure that it will make a profit. Individuals can beat the respective houses with winning numbers and longer than expected life spans, but, on average, whole groups of gamblers and an-nuity purchasers do not. Therein lies the profitability of both businesses.

The profit needs of commercial life insurance companies sig-nificantly affect annuity payout rates. For example, the Connecticut Teachers' Retirement System, the defined benefit pension plan for public schools, is able to offer a supplementary nonprofit annuity to its members with a payout rate of 8.7 percent that is significantly higher than the commercial market rate of 6.8 percent for males and 6.1 per-cent for females.

Since women live on average two years longer than men, they will collect annuity payments that much longer. To compensate for making more payments to women, issuers of commercial annuities lessen each of their payments. Unlike DB plans that may sell annuities to their members, commercial insurance companies are allowed to practice gender discrimination in their annuity rates. While this discrimination may make sense actuarially, it does not make human or social sense. We can safely assume that the annual cost of living for women is not less than that for men. It is also true that rich people live longer than poor people, but commercial life insurance companies do not use that as a reason to lessen their payout rates.

People who believe they are going to live a long time purchase an-nuities more often than people who don't; and they do, on average, live longer. They collect their payments longer, making them more expensive than normal longevity rates would suggest. Commercial insurance companies compensate for what they call "adverse selection" into the risk pools by increasing all longevity assumptions and thereby lowering payout rates. Because participation in Social Security and most defined benefit pension funds is mandatory, the problem of adverse selection is avoided and they can base payments on normal longevity assumptions, resulting in higher payout rates than commercial annuities.

The costs of private annuities vary widely, reflecting the types and amounts of costs that are embedded within them. According to a Congressional Budget Office study, "marketing costs can be substantial since annuities constitute a relatively complicated product with a large number of options generally requiring contracting with commissioned agents to explain and sell annuity products." Commissions for such services can range from 1 percent to 12 percent. Extra overhead costs, which include profits, for private annuities make them between 8 percent and 13 percent more expensive than they otherwise would be. A large source of the extra cost, according to the study, is the effect of adverse selection.[29]

FANTASY OWNERSHIP

In sum, 401(k) and other defined contribution plans deliver inferior results for retirees compared to defined benefit traditional pensions for four general reasons:

- Low contributions.
- Drain-off during the accumulation and spend-down phases of considerable administrative fees, commissions, and profits by the financial services industry.
- Participants bearing all the risks of investing.
- Lack of the full social insurance advantage of risk pooling.

Not only are DC plans much less predictable and adequate in terms of benefit amounts than DB plans, contrary to widespread beliefs, they are more expensive to fund for comparable levels of benefits. They lack the full advantages of risk pooling and have significant drain-offs of management fees, commissions, and profits, making them less efficient in providing for income replacement during retirement. A dollar invested in a DB plan will inevitably produce far more in terms of retirement benefits than a dollar invested in a DC plan as numerous studies and our own experience in Connecticut have shown.[30] For me, both the employer' and employees' contributions for the DC plan were more than double that of the DB one, which delivered much higher retirement income.

The financial services industry encourages the belief that participants can do it all with these accounts. They can finance their retirements, have rainy-day funds for unexpected expenses, and have money to leave to children or other heirs. But each use of the savings for non-retirement expenditures is at the expense of their ostensible purpose. If they do not produce enough accumulations to adequately support retirement alone, they certainly don't produce enough to support retirement along with emergency expenditures and provision of inheritances to children as well.

With the rise of 401(k) and other defined contribution plans, the financial services industry has gained control of a substantial amount of worker retirement savings and turned them into vehicles for its own profit needs. Those in turn have limited the ability of workers to accumulate sufficient savings for retirement security. In return for the loss of their retirement security, workers have been left with a fantasy notion of ownership. It is *their* money in the private accounts, but workers have only abstract ownership. Robin Blackburn refers to these savings as gray capital.[31] In theory, it is capital individually owned by participants. In reality, the financial services industry exercises most of the privileges of ownership. It holds the capital. It invests it. It draws profits off it. As a result, paying into the accounts is like paying for a house that someone else will be living in at minimal rent until you retire. You own what someone else—in this case, the financial services industry—gets to use. Then, after retirement, the financial services industry issues you a kind of reverse mortgage on your accumulation.

With private accounts, participants save for retirement—the ostensible purpose—and support the profit needs of the financial services industry at the same time. This is a contradictory set of goals. They can't adequately save for retirement and simultaneously support the financial services industry. The financial services industry, on the other hand, is able to accomplish its goals with these accounts by combining all it appropriates from each individual one.

This problem goes beyond the drain-off of savings by the financial services industry. Even if the drain-off was reduced to a bare minimum of necessary administrative expenses, the accounts would still come up short in terms of providing adequate support for retirement. The deeper problem is with the individualized approach that negates all of the pooling advantages of social insurance. For that reason, well-meaning reforms such as seeking to make 401(k) fee charges lower and more transparent will do little to resolve the deeper crisis in retirement security.

Do defined contribution plans have any advantages over defined benefit plans? Yes, there are two advantages, but they come at very high costs. DC plans are portable. Workers can generally roll them over from job to job. That is a very important advantage, especially since the labor force is increasingly mobile, with most people changing jobs many times over their careers. Some DB plans can also be rolled over into other DB plans. In the public sector, a state may have reciprocity agreements with one or more other states to accept each other's plans. But that is rare for DB plans, with the exception of Social Security. Because Social Security is a national system, it is completely portable. All that matters is whether the employer participates in it, and almost all are legally obliged to. The portability disadvantage of an employer-based DB plan could be remedied through development of a national association of such plans.

The other advantage of DC plans is that children can inherit accumulations within them. DB plans provide support for surviving spouses, but usually not children. If the DC participant dies before retirement or shortly after retirement, the accumulation in the account goes to heirs. As we've seen, this may be important to individuals. But from the point of view of policy—that is, national policy on retirement—it contradicts the whole notion and advantages of social insurance.

With DC plans, the whole purpose is to create individual wealth. If you retire at age sixty-five with a DC plan and you die one month later, that money will go to your heirs. It will not go to support other retirees. For some people, that's an important advantage because they want to be able to leave money to children or other heirs. The problem is that you can't do both. You can't both create individual wealth or turn retirement into a way of creating individual wealth and at the same time adequately support retirement.

While giving money to heirs is something that many people may want to do, from a retirement social insurance principle, it is irrational. It results in transferring money from the third age to the second age. Money originally intended for the support of retired people will be given to people in their working ages, who are earning money and do not need it, providing a windfall to people who are at the point when they are capable of earning money. Windfalls, of course, are very nice for their recipients. But such windfalls drain off funds that could otherwise be used to support the third age.

CHAPTER 6

A Model Unravels

In 1999, five years after the publication of its seminal *Averting the Old Age Crisis*, the World Bank's then chief economist and later Nobel Prize recipient, Joseph Stiglitz, along with Peter R. Orszag, revisited the report's main recipe for retirement system reform. At a World Bank conference in Washington, DC, they delivered a crushing critique of the 1994 reform model with their paper, "Rethinking Pension Reform: Ten Myths About Social Security Systems." They focused on the report's advocacy of a dominant private, mandatory, defined contribution pillar, arguing that it was built on ten myths:

1. Individual accounts raise national savings. 2. Rates of return are higher under individual accounts. 3. Declining rates of return on pay-as-you-go systems reflect fundamental problems. 4. Investment of public trust funds in equities has no macroeconomic effects. 5. Labor market incentives are better under individual accounts. 6. Defined benefit plans necessarily provide more of an incentive to retire early. 7. Competition ensures low administrative costs under individual accounts. 8. Corrupt and inefficient governments provide a rationale for individual accounts. 9. Bailout politics are worse under public defined benefit plans. 10. Investment of public trust funds is always squandered and mismanaged.[1]

Of these criticisms, it is worth emphasizing myth 2: that individual accounts produce higher rates of return than defined benefit ones under pay-as-you-go systems, and myth 7: that competition ensures low administrative costs for them. Those, especially the claim of higher returns, were repeated endlessly as justifications for involuntary trans fers or bait for voluntary transfers to individual accounts. The two are connected because high administrative fees are one cause for low rates of return for defined contribution individual accounts.

Orszag and Stiglitz note that mainstream institutions such as the *Financial Times*—not just conservative think tanks like Cato—repeated the belief that individual accounts would produce higher rates of return than pay-as-you-go systems such as Social Security. Those comparisons, though, confuse gross with net rates of return. Administrative costs reduce gross rates of return for individuals, and, as we have seen, they are considerable. The authors conclude that the underlying costs of decentralized private systems with multiple providers (banks, insurance companies, investment firms) overseeing different individual accounts make it much more expensive than a centralized government-run system. The underlying costs include "sales and marketing cost, fund management charges, regulatory and compliance costs, record-keeping, and adverse selection effects."[2] Those costs amounted to "between 40 and 45 percent of the value of individual accounts in the United Kingdom."[3]

Transition costs add another layer that is often ignored in comparisons. If a full pay-as-you-go system such as Social Security were to suddenly be stopped, with new workers being placed in 401(k)-like accounts, retirees under the old system would still be owed incomes. Without new workers making contributions, the gap would have to be made up somehow. Unless the government reneged on its promises to retirees, which is unlikely because of the political crisis it would cause, it would have to raise taxes or transfer money from other budgets to make up for the liabilities attached to the old system.

Orszag and Stiglitz made additional points. In a pure pay-as-you-go system, there is no investment income. All income is from contributions. Individual accounts invest contributions so that they have income from both the contributions and the investment returns on them. By implication, any pay-as-you-go system could make a transition to one that also made investments, as is the case with private and public state and local defined benefit pension systems. The increased rate of return owing to investments thus does not have to be achieved by transferring to individual 401(k) accounts. In addition, a pay-as-you-go system does not have prefunding—that is, have a surplus large enough to pay out all that is owed to current and retired workers if contributions were to completely stop. Prefunding adds additional money that can be invested and produce a higher rate of return. As the authors put it, "it is the additional funding, not the individual accounts themselves, that is crucial to producing the higher rate of return."[4]

Also to be considered is the redistribution component of a pay-as-you-go system like Social Security. Its payout formula is moderately skewed to favor lower-income groups that receive higher rates of return than higher-income groups as a means to decrease elderly poverty. Rates of return thus vary according to income. The variation, though, is mild compared to that of individual investment accounts. The concept of unpredictable volatility much better captures the latter variation. In addition to the normal risks of investment with business cycle and individual portfolio ups and downs, there is a timing risk. Orszag and Stiglitz cited a Brookings Institute study about hypothetical workers who invested 2 percent of their earnings in stock index funds over forty-year careers. The study showed that "workers reaching age 62 in 1968 would have enjoyed a 39 percent replacement rate (that is, the monthly benefit from their retirement annuity would equal 39 percent of prior wages) from their investments. By contrast, the replacement rate for workers retiring in 1974—only six years later—would have been only 17 percent, or less than half as much."[5]

Public defined benefit systems have an advantage over individual accounts in that their investment risks can be spread over a longer time period. Individuals only have the length of their careers to ride out stock market dips in order to end up with overall gains. Governments are not so restricted because they outlive individuals. As Orszag and Stiglitz put it, "a public defined benefit system can spread risk across generations in a way that is not possible under a private defined contribution program."[6]

Despite the scathing critique, the World Bank didn't change course, and shortly after delivering the presentation, which surely left his colleagues stunned and dismayed, Stiglitz was forced out of his bank position. Today, the World Bank includes links to over three thousand bank and non-bank pension-related reports, articles, and papers, but the Orszag and Stiglitz "Ten Myths" article isn't among them

Stiglitz might be considered the anti-Friedman among top economists. He has consistently argued against Friedman's market fundamentalism by reaffirming the Keynesian position that significant government fiscal interventions and regulations are needed to keep the system functioning well and to prevent or minimize crises. That, however, doesn't make him the complete anti-Friedman. Such a position could only be occupied by a Marxist economist who argued for complete government control. Nevertheless, in the current spectrum of economic policy in the United States, his and Friedman's positions are about as far apart as practically possible. It is a space prominently shared with Paul Krugman, the Princeton economist, *New York Times* columnist, and fellow Nobel laureate.[7]

The trajectory of Stiglitz's career, including his critical intervention into retirement policy, reveals the competing pulls of professional integrity, economic and political power, and personal principles. No one denies his skill as an economist, which was reflected in his meteoric career rise with positions at the elite universities MIT, Yale, Stanford, Oxford, Cambridge, Princeton, and Columbia. Top university economists are often tapped for political appointments, to move from teaching to making economic policy. Bill Clinton invited him to join his Council of Economic Advisers as a member and later chair in 1993. In 1997, he transferred to the World Bank as its chief economist, shifting from overseeing economic policy in the leading country to overseeing it for the whole world.

But the move to the World Bank may have represented less a promotion than a way for the Clinton administration to rid itself of an uncomfortable internal critic. Clinton's New Democrats, who supported Third Way policies, did not include Stiglitz. Instead, they practiced exceptionally Wall Street–friendly policies, from engineering approval of NAFTA, to the repeal of the Glass-Steagall Act, which kept commercial and investment banks separate, to flirting with Social Security privatization. The financial services industry, which rewards Democratic as well as Republican candidates for good conduct with campaign contributions, found that it could actually accomplish more with Democrats than Republicans in office. That the Democrats were rhetorically the critics of Wall Street gave them political legitimacy to do what the Republicans couldn't. The reality was thus one of lip service to anti–Wall Street populism, while quietly working with Wall Street lobbyists.

But Stiglitz chose not to cooperate. He had enough stature as a leading economist on his way to becoming a Nobel laureate to be immune to fears of the economic consequences of losing jobs. He could afford to be independent minded and vocal in a way that didn't diminish his integrity.

Stiglitz remains an outlier, an uncomfortable pariah to Democratic Party power brokers and insiders. He will not play the game, but he cannot be dismissed or marginalized easily, given his international stature. Just as Richard Nixon used to dread opening the *Washington Post* every day, fearing how he would be skewered in a Herblock cartoon, Obama's insider economists must fear or swear softly over what Stiglitz might say in the press, along with the near-daily criticism from Krugman's *New York Times* columns.

Orszag's trajectory has been quite different from Stiglitiz's. Since writing "Rethinking Pension Reform" in 1999, he occupied a number of public and private positions, including being a senior fellow at the Brookings Institute and director of the Congressional Budget Office. In 2005, he staked out a position on Social Security that was between the World Bank's view that it be reduced to only an antipoverty backup program for retirement provision and the defenders, who sought to maintain or expand its benefits. He and economist and Social Security specialist Peter A. Diamond, in arguing against the Bush plan to divert part of the contributions into private accounts, called instead for reducing benefits, with the greatest reductions for the highest-earning groups. They argued that those reductions would be the fairest because higher-earning groups lived longer than lower-earning ones. They did not mention that it would undermine political support for Social Security from the upper-middle class.

In 2009, President Obama named Orszag director of the Office of Budget and Management. Orszag resigned that position in July 2010. In November 2010, consistent with his 2005 paper with Diamond, he endorsed the main conclusion of the Simpson-Bowles Commission, established by President Obama in 2010 to address the national debt, which sought to reduce Social Security benefits. Three weeks later in December, he took a position as vice president of global banking at Citigroup, a position that normally pays, according to the *New York Times*, between $2 million and $3 million.[8]

Orszag was able to parlay his top but modest-paying federal positions into a lucrative private career, as have many others in the revolving door between top public and private positions. One need not be a conspiracy theorist to suspect that people in top public positions with goals of higher future incomes mold their views and actions so that they will be attractive to private employers. As economist Dean Baker wrote, "Orszag and others in a similar situation undoubtedly understand how the positions they take in their roles in government can affect their future career options [including] the prospect of big-paying jobs on Wall Street and elsewhere."[9] In an article titled "In Money-Changers We Trust," journalist Robert Scheer wrote that Peter Orszag represents a striking example "of the synergy between big government and high finance."[10]

Orszag and Stiglitz wrote their criticism of the World Bank in 1999 when the stock market had not reached the end of its ten-year spectacular rise during which the Dow Jones average climbed from 2,342 to 11,497, nearly five times as high. If market-based individual accounts were going to do well at any time, it was then. Yet Orszag and Stiglitz found, contrary to conventional claims, that their rates of return were lower than those of pay-as-you-go systems, including Social Security. The rise in the stock market stopped abruptly with the burst of the tech stock bubble and the crash after the September 11, 2001, terrorist attacks. It regained some momentum after 2006 but then sank steeply with the 2008 recession. As a result, Dow Jones averages in 2010 were no higher than they were in 2000, a decade of no overall growth. If Orszag and Stiglitz's conclusion was valid at a time when there was a run-up of stock market values with no end in sight, it was even more valid after ten years of no overall growth, as was shown by a 2008 National Institute on Retirement Security study cited earlier, as well as my own experiences.[11]

The belief that private accounts would deliver higher rates of return than occupational defined benefit plans or Social Security began to wither with the stagnant returns of the stock market in the first decade of the new century. The ideological and actual purveyors of these accounts pleaded patience. The market would come back, they argued. They pleaded for more contributions. Save more to ensure your retirement security. They pleaded fatalistic acceptance. There is no realistic alternative to private accounts. They sought to expand their failing model with a partial takeover of Social Security.

When a quarter or more of retirement savings in private accounts such as 401(k)s evaporated nearly overnight with the 2008 recession, it became more difficult for the financial services industry to cover up the unfolding disaster in retirement security. In the public consciousness, 401(k)s had shifted from an enticing opportunity for substantial private wealth creation to an inferior retirement plan. "I *just* have a 401(k)" became the new sobering realization. Or, in a new focus for gallows humor, "My 401(k) is now a 201(k)." Not only did people lose money, they also lost time—the time it would take to make up the losses and time in retirement. Pity the people who were planning on retiring that year. They either had to retire into less income than they had expected or keep working.

THE UK "MIS-SELLING" SCANDAL

In their 1999 paper, Orszag and Stiglitz had cited the high administrative costs of personal accounts in the United Kingdom. There is
another cautionary tale from that country, what came to be known
as the "mis-selling scandal." The Thatcher government's privatization
and conversion of pension provision was off to a roaring start in 1988.
The financial services industry aggressively marketed the so-called
personal pensions as the government pursued its carrot-and-stick
policy to encourage people to transfer to them. It offered generous
tax rebates as incentives and reduced State Earnings-Related Pension
Scheme (SERPS—the national retirement system) benefits. Legions
of salespeople pounded on doors promising spectacular stock market gains. Within three years, over 4 million people contracted out
of their government or employer-based pensions for personal pension
plans.[12] The "personal pensions," like all defined contribution plans,
were based on building up stock market investment portfolios to individually finance retirement income. They replaced defined benefit
plans that had guaranteed benefits based on lengths of service and
final salary amounts.

What seemed to be a very successful start for the Conservative
government's retirement reform proved, though, to be the start of
something unintended and deeply embarrassing: the largest financial
scandal in British history. The warning bells began to sound when the
government realized that the program was costing it more than it was
saving. The cost of the tax rebates to encourage people to contract out
of SERPS exceeded what was being saved by no longer having them
within the system. Far more serious was the exposé that the financial
services industry, with its aggressive sales tactics, was convincing people to leave public and employer defined benefit pensions for inferior
personal plans.

Government regulators then stepped in. They required that those
who had been mis-sold private plans be reinstated to their occupational pensions, if they had them, or compensated for the financial
damage. Reinstatement became a knotty problem requiring calculation

of the cost of compensating the funds for the time lost during the contracted-out period, a bone of contention between the fund managers and the liable insurance companies that had sold the private plans. For those who had contracted out of SERPS, reinstatement for time going forward was not an issue because the original legislation had allowed for contracting back in. What was of issue was credit for the time during the contracted-out period, which the system did not allow. For that, the insurance companies were required to pay compensation. By 1999, the insurance companies had paid out $17 billion in compensation to victims plus fines.[13]

THE CHILEAN MODEL FAILS

Orszag and Stiglitz also cited the problem of high administrative fees in Chile's privatized system. That was just one of the problems. Because Chilean privatization was so important in this history, I decided that it required my first visit to the country.

I flew into Chile with a lot of memories. The 1973 coup and its repercussions were formative events for me when I was in my late twenties. I had worked with Chile support groups for a long time at the various teaching posts and took part in demonstrations, including one organized by exiles at a talk that Milton Friedman gave in 1978 to a business group in San Francisco. I helped to arrange talks by exiles throughout the period of the dictatorship until it ended in 1990. By that time, the exiles I knew had settled in the United States with families and jobs. It was not so easy for them to return to Chile where jobs were not waiting and with children who were growing up with different roots. Reluctantly, most of them stayed in the United States.

I continued to be involved in Chilean issues, and in my courses on Latin America, I always taught about what had happened in Chile and what it represented. But I had never visited the country. Now I would visit it in a new context. If before my relationship to Chile had been out of solidarity with people who I respected, who had been smashed by a military dictatorship—something that I had fortunately never experienced in the United States—now I had a common connection: the experience of being trapped in a similar type of retirement system that did not work. The Chilean system was imposed with bayonets; we were swindled into ours. As Woody Guthrie sang, "Some men will rob you with a six gun, others with a fountain pen." The result was the same.

As preparation for my trip, I searched the Internet for references to the Chilean system and encountered a lot of fog. Most references seemed to be positive or neutral. You really needed to know where to look to get to the heart of the matter. Fortunately, through Chilean contacts, I learned about the National Center for Alternative Development (CENDA). Its vice president, Manuel Riesco, is an expert on the Chilean retirement system, and his writings were as useful as they were critical.

What astounded me was that much of what Riesco was describing in Chile, we were experiencing in Connecticut: entrapment in a system that delivered less than half the benefits of traditional pensions while costing more and being enormously profitable for the financial services industry. To top it off, the Dutch multinational financial corporation ING that administered our system also played a major role in the privatized Chilean system.

In Chile, the people that I met are aware of the inequity of the Administradoras de Fondos de Pensiones (AFP), the name of their privatized system. When I told them that, in the early 1980s, people in the United States were sold on the idea that they would make much more money from 401(k)s than traditional pensions, they smiled. It was the same in Chile. The AFPs started with the same promise. At a birthday party of mostly professors from the University of Chile, I was introduced as in the country to study the AFPs. Their faces contorted, and almost in unison, they responded, "Don't copy our system." Upon arriving, I met a man who had a degenerative, terminal disease. He retired under the AFP three years earlier, but the income was insufficient, so he had to return to work six hundred miles away from his family in order to support them. He was a perfect symbol of the failure of Chile's retirement system. His final months would be spent working and sick, not because he was a workaholic but because, despite many years of hard work and contributing to the AFP system, the benefits were too low to support him.

I also met people who were retired under the old Instituto de Normalización Previsional (INP) system. The same age as the man with terminal disease, they were actually retired and appeared to be comfortable. They said that, in 1980 and 1981, there was a lot of pressure on them to shift to the new AFP system, but they resisted and were very glad that they had.

I was shown around and introduced to people by Ximena de la Barra. She was a tireless woman who was forced out of the country in 1975 and then worked for many years for the United Nations before retirement. She returned to the country after the fall of the dictatorship. She has not really retired, because she kept up a breathtaking level of activity going to meetings and writing.

At dusk, we wound our way through a section of beach houses stretched up a hill overlooking the Pacific near Isla Negra. Ximena was driving and got lost. "Don't worry," she said, "I always get there eventually." We were looking for the house of Orlando Caputo and Graciela Galarce. Ximena was on a mission to get their signatures on a permission form to publish their article on the Chilean copper industry in a book that she edited and translated. I wanted to meet the man who was the antithesis of José Piñera. He had been the general manager of CODELCO, the nationalized copper company, which Piñera had substantially reprivatized, leaving only enough in public hands to support the military.

After doubling back from several dead-ends, we arrived. In May in the late Chilean fall, most of the summer houses were empty. Caputo and Galarce lived in a small house with two small woodstoves for heat. Intended for summer weather, the walls were not more than two inches thick, not even the depth of a two-by-four. They need the stoves. The house was not their summer house, but their only house. (I wondered how many houses Piñera had.)

Caputo took us up to the second floor where there was one large room, a room that any academic who works hard at writing would understand. There were stacks of books and papers everywhere in no particular order. Galarce asked what we would like to drink. Wine would be the normal fare in this very Chilean place, but Caputo said that they still have work to do that evening. Coffee was the drink.

I learned that they were at Universidad Nacional Autónoma de México at the same time I was. We knew many of the same people and even lived in Copilco, a neighborhood that borders the sprawling university campus.

I told Caputo that I was researching the AFP and showed him our group's website. He put it in his computer's favorites list so that he could look at it later. Then he said he had something to show me. After some rummaging around in a back room, he returned with a book about the AFP written by a former student of his who was of German origin, Doris Elter, who tragically died in a plane crash in Peru in 1996. The book was based on her thesis, directed by Caputo, at the Universidad Arcis.[14]

Since the book had been published eleven years earlier, we wondered whether I would be able to buy a copy somewhere. Caputo said the book was crucial for my understanding of the AFP fraud, but it was his only copy. At this time, I did not know that it was special to him. It contained a prologue he had written, a memorial to his student. Nevertheless he gave me the book. I decided to search for a copy to buy in Santiago. If that failed, I would take his book back to the United States, photocopy it, and then return it to him. He put a lot of trust in someone he had just met; I'm not sure that I would have loaned a special book as easily. (Within two days, the untiring Ximena located a copy at a bookstore, and Caputo's copy was safely returned to him.)

As we left, Caputo showed me the view down the hillside of empty summer houses. I asked him if he felt isolated here. He said no, pointing to the computer. He had just posted an article on the financial crisis on an international website that he wanted me to see.

He and Graciela were living their retirement in a modest house supported by a combined $800 "exonerated" pension that the government, as a result of legislative action, made available to people dismissed from their jobs for political reasons during the dictatorship. Financially modest, it was a highly symbolic attempt to address a historical debt to people who survived, but whose lives were turned upside down.

I thought of José Piñera who continues to live in very comfortable circumstances. He has so much wealth that he does not need a retirement plan. He will be forever known in Chile as the man who expropriated other people's retirement plans. Caputo and Galarce, though, have something that he, with all of his wealth and high-level contacts, will never be able to obtain: a clear conscience.

Until the mid-1990s, no one questioned Chile's AFP privatized retirement system. Not even the dictatorship's harshest critics or professional researchers knew how bad it was. That was because no one had yet retired under the new system; everyone was still in the accumulation phase. As in the United States, few people had any idea how much money they had to accumulate to retire securely.

Elter was one of the first critical analysts of the privatized system from within Chile. In her 1995 doctoral thesis, which Caputo directed, she presented her criticisms:

1. The administrators of the AFP were claiming average growth rates of 11 percent. Elter concluded that the real long-term growth rate was between 3 percent and 6 percent. The AFP's exaggerated claims resulted from methodological errors and projecting short-term growth (1982–1992) under artificially favorable conditions into the future. The 1982–1992 period favored high growth rates for capital because of the massive privatizations carried out by the dictatorship. That period would not repeat itself. You can only sell the farm once.

2. While the vast majority of working Chileans would pay into the AFP system at various times during their working lives, they would not all make enough payments to be eligible to collect pensions. Elter estimated that only 52 percent would be eligible to collect, compared to the 71 percent in the previous system. That was because the Chilean economy did not

support long-term stable employment. Many people moved in and out of formal economy jobs where AFP deductions were made, having long periods when deductions were not made. It was common, for example, for factory workers to be laid off during economic downturns. These laid-off workers would turn to selling products in informal street markets in order to obtain incomes.

3. Elter projected that the AFP rate of income substitution would be lower than that of the INP system. Whereas the old system was providing an average retirement income of 75 percent of final salary, the new system would deliver between 51 percent and 72 percent for men and 27 percent and 36 percent for women.

4. Elter especially emphasized, as the previous point demonstrated, that the AFP system was prejudicial against women.

In his memorial prologue to the book, which came out after her death, Caputo cast Elter's analysis in the framework of a classic opposition between the interests of capital and labor. The AFP system, he wrote, contains

forced savings of workers that shore up the financing of companies and the economy that has enabled for many years high growth rates . . . from which industrial and financial business interests have obtained high profits. But when the stock market falls, the AFP investments act as a brake to avoid a complete collapse. At the same time, the rich opportunely withdraw their investments, leaving it to the workers' retirement savings to take the hit.[15]

Shortly after Elter submitted her 1995 thesis, Manuel Riesco and Hugo Fazo were presenting the findings of CENDA research on a radio program. It aired on Tuesdays at 11:00 a.m., when most people were at work. Their few listeners were overwhelmingly housewives and retired people. One day, they received a letter from a listener who presented figures to prove that the AFP represented a giant robbery. Riesco glanced at it before filing it away to respond to later. After several months, he pulled the letter from his briefcase and studied the figures. He could find nothing wrong with them. He showed them to colleagues and they couldn't find anything wrong. The retired listener was right.[16]

The CENDA researchers, with Riesco in the lead, then began to study the AFP seriously. In 2005, the INP contracted CENDA to carry out further studies of the AFP. That gave them access to all of the government information. The CENDA researchers now had access to more information than had Elter; timing also presented them with new information. In the interval between her study and theirs, there had been significant contractions in the world economy, in particular, the 1997 Asian financial crisis.

In all important respects, their findings confirmed hers: (1) real growth rates for the AFP funds were a lot less than those originally projected by the plan sponsors; (2) retirees under AFP were receiving less than half of what those under the old INP system received; (3) coverage was less in the new system since so many participants, due to the nature of the Chilean economy, did not have the minimum number of contributions to qualify for pensions; (4) there was a significant gap between retirement annuities paid to men and to women.[17]

In addition, they documented that the corporations managing the AFP were pocketing one of every three pesos deposited and accumulated in them. This occurred during both the accumulation and spend-down annuity phases.

Thus, by 2000, it was well known in Chile that the AFP system was a failure in its ostensible purpose: to provide adequate income security for retirees. That, however, did not stop backers of the system from claiming success. In December 2004, as the debate over partially privatizing Social Security was heating up the United States, José Piñera published an op-ed opinion article in the *New York Times* praising the system as an unqualified success that presented "an opportunity for a bipartisan agreement in the United States in this crucial area of public policy."[18] What he was referring to was the flirtation with the idea of Social Security privatization by certain Democratic Party officials as well as Republicans who had long been sold on the idea. He explained how the AFP system worked and would be a model for US Social Security privatization, but was short on figures about how it turned out for retirees. He implied that Chileans now embraced the system and "workers cheer the stock market's surges." He closed the article with, "When workers feel that they themselves own a part of their country's wealth, they become participants and supporters of a free market and a free society." Praising support for "a free society" was a strange comment, coming from a man who had been a key official in a military dictatorship.

When Riesco at CENDA learned of Piñera's praise of the AFP system in the *Times*, he immediately prepared a detailed response in which he repeated the two most damning facts about the new system: retirees were receiving less than half as much as they would have under the old INP system, and one of every three pesos that workers contributed was being siphoned out by the companies running the system.

The *Times* declined to publish it, but a couple of weeks later its reporter, Larry Rohter, appeared at the CENDA office carrying the submitted article.[19] He spent the day with the CENDA researchers, conducted additional research and interviews, and then published a page-one article in the *Times* on January 27, 2005, titled, "Chile's Retirees Find Shortfall in Private Plan." Rohter reported the damning information and discussed at length how the AFP investments had a favorable effect on growth rates. "What we have is a system that is good for Chile," said a government official who spoke on condition of anonymity, "but bad for most Chileans." Piñera declined repeated requests to be interviewed for the article.

Three months later, John Tierney, one of the *Times*' conservative columnists, made a "pilgrimage" to Santiago, Chile, to supposedly find answers to the Social Security debate in the United States. He found what he was looking for: a ringing endorsement of the AFP system. He concluded that if the United States replaced its Social Security system with an AFP-like plan, retirees would be able to replace 90 percent of their preretirement income.[20] Tierney's cheery report flew completely in the face of all the facts that showed that they were replacing far less than 50 percent. But his purpose was to convince rather than enable understanding. Of course, Tierney's report was based on ideologically driven speculation rather than empirical evidence, but it was masterful in achieving its desired effect: to plant doubt in people's minds about Social Security and thereby pave the way for acceptance of privatization.

In 2005, during Chile's presidential campaign, CNN in Spanish broadcast a debate among the presidential candidates across Latin America. Many viewers outside Chile were shocked to learn that the central topic was the failure of the privatized retirement system to deliver adequate income security. That system had been held up as the model for reforms in their own countries. Now none of the candidates were defending it. Even Sebastian Piñera from the right-wing National Renewal Party and brother of the system's designer, agreed that it needed serious reform. The efforts of CENDA and others to expose the system's failure had borne fruit.

Riesco of CENDA had great hope that out of the crisis would come a reestablishment of the INP defined benefit system as the basis for all Chileans, as it had been before José Piñera and the Chicago Boys had been able to use dictatorial conditions to impose their ideas on the country. That was his hope, but it was not to be. On April 4, 2006, he presented CENDA's proposal for an overhaul of the Chilean retirement system to President Michelle Bachelet's Advisory Commission on Retirement Reform. It advocated a system of three pillars. The first would be a guaranteed minimum pension for old age or disability paid out of general tax revenues. The second, the largest part, would be a defined benefit pension based on employee contributions. The third, the smallest part, would be individual savings that would function like the current AFP.[21]

In 2008, the Chilean Congress passed Law 20.255, which reformed the national retirement system. The AFPs were left in place as the main basis. Instead of topping off defined benefit pensions with individual savings via the AFP system, as CENDA advocated, the reformed system topped off individual savings via the AFPs with government-supplied funds to bring them up to minimum levels. To resolve the problem of so many people not having enough contributions within the AFP system to qualify for any pension, the reform created Basic Solidarity Pensions—minimum monthly pensions of US$140 that would be paid by the IPN—the old defined benefit system that would now be called the Instituto de Previsión Social (Institute for Social Funding, IPS). To support those whose AFP annuities were insufficient, the IPS would provide a supplement—the Aporte Previsional Solidario (Solidarity Fund Contribution). On a sliding scale, this would provide up to $374 to those who received less than $477 from their AFP annuities and were in the poorest 60 percent. That is, up to 60 percent of Chileans could potentially qualify for the supplementary pension.[22]

There is no question that the reform provided much-needed relief for the profound failures of the AFP system. But it did not resolve the fundamental problem of that system. Essentially, the reform used public money to alleviate the worst outcomes of the AFP system; and public money would have to continue being used to subsidize continuation of that system, money that would then be unavailable for other social expenses such as health, education, or poverty alleviation. The reform was in line with the World Bank's formula. It kept the system of individual capitalization as a source of capital accumulation for businesses, in general, and high profits for the financial services industry, in particular, while using public money to douse a smoldering social explosion of elderly poverty.

REVERSING PRIVATIZATION

Argentina achieved fame in the 1990s as the Latin American country that had most toed the line of neoliberal reforms. Then-president Carlos Menem, a member of the Peronist Justicialista Party, enthusiastically embraced and promoted neoliberal reforms that included privatizing state enterprises and adopting the US dollar as the currency. In what one newspaper called "the mother of all privatizations," it substantially privatized its public retirement system in 1993 with World Bank encouragement.[23]

The 1993 reform created three tiers. The first tier was a guaranteed minimum public pension for men over sixty-five and women over sixty with thirty years of contributions. The second tier provided a guaranteed pension based on number of years and amount of contributions before 1994, when the reform went into effect. The third tier was made up of all employee contributions beginning in 1994. Workers could choose to have them credited to the existing public defined benefit or newly created private defined contribution plans. The rules specified that anyone could change at any time from the public to the private system, but once in the private system, they could not change back. As new workers came into the workforce, the third tier would progressively make up more of the source of retirement income.

As with the Chilean AFPs and Mexican AFIOREs, different, supposedly competing, private financial services corporations—Administradoras de Foldos de Jubilaciones y Pensiones (AFJPs)—administered the private plans. The new AFJPs aggressively promoted their plans, implying that workers would do much better under them than in the traditional public pension plan. Their advertising campaigns convinced upward of 82 percent of existing and new workers to choose the private plans.[24]

The AFJP industry took off in the middle 1990s as the Argentine economy was going through a growth spurt due to the privatization of state-owned businesses that was attracting domestic and international investments. But, as in Chile, you can only sell the farm once. By 2001, the privatization growth spurt had spent itself and the economy spectacularly crashed, taking down with it accumulated personal savings in the AFJPs. The crash produced a social explosion and multiple political crises. Over a three-week period in late 2001 and early 2002, Argentina had three different presidents. The country began to stabilize with the election of Néstor Kirchner, a center-left Peronist, in 2003. The next election, in 2007, was won overwhelmingly by his wife, Cristina Fernández de Kirchner.

Though the Kirchners were from the same political party as Carlos Menem, who was responsible for the privatization binge, they saw the need to use public investments, regulations, and programs to contain and reverse the crisis. They modified or completely reversed many of the Menem administration's neoliberal reforms. In this context, they began to have serious reservations about what had been wrought by the 1993 pension privatization.

There were two sides of the damage: what it was doing to retiree income and what it was doing to government financial capability. In terms of the former, as with all cases where defined contribution plans replace defined benefit ones, eventually participants realize that they will get much less income under the new system than they would have under the old. As the realization grew, trade unions began to take up the issue. "For me the AFJP are one of the greatest swindles ever perpetrated on the Argentinean people," stated Hugo Moyano, secretary general of the General Confederation of Labor, known as the CGT by its Spanish acronym, the largest labor union in the country.[25]

The other issue was the potential damage that the system was doing to the country. Both domestic and foreign AFJP administrators were increasingly investing the funds abroad. Instead of the funds spurring domestic growth, they were being siphoned out of the country. The rationale was that the administrators were searching for higher rates of return that would benefit retirees directly. But, at the same time, domestic investment would benefit the national economy more and therefore retirees indirectly. The system also produced the strange situation in which money from the retirement funds that the government earlier controlled to loan or invest for national purposes was now in the hands of the AFJPs to loan to the government, shifting the government from being a creditor to a debtor.

In 2006, the ministry of labor determined that 250,000 teachers, judges, and others in the private plans had been ineligible to join them and transferred them back to the public plan.[26] Their guaranteed pensions were calculated as if they had never left the public plan. Then, on February 13, 2007, the Senate voted unanimously for a reform that would allow participants in the AFJP a 180-day window of opportunity once every five years to switch to the public plan. Members of the public plan would continue to have the option to switch to the private plan at any time. When the time for retirement came, pensions would be calculated proportionately according to what had been invested in the different plans. The House of Deputies passed the measure two weeks later.

Once the measure became law, the first window of opportunity was scheduled for April 13 to December 31, 2007. There was considerable speculation about how many participants would have second thoughts about the AFJP and switch. On the first day, forty-eight thousand changed, including former President Néstor Kirchner.[27]

The AFJPs did not openly oppose the new law, but they heavily tried to convince their members to stay put. They were ready on the first day of the window of opportunity with an online simulator that members could use to compare their likely benefits under the private and public systems. Not surprisingly, the simulations almost inevitably showed them doing better under the private system. The online simulations offered different scenarios. Those who entered the AFJPs at age fifty-five would receive about the same as in the public plan; those who entered at forty would receive 27 percent more income; and those who entered at twenty-five would receive a whopping two-and-a-half times the retirement income of the public pension.[28]

The government agency that regulated AFJPs immediately criticized the simulations as being loaded with unrealistically optimistic assumptions about how investments would fare. In the middle of August, it ordered that the simulator be taken offline.[29] But the damage had already been done. Many who had already used the simulator remained convinced that they would fare better with their private plans. Others were confused by the conflicting messages coming from the AFJPs and the government and did nothing, thereby remaining in the private plans.

By the end of the window of opportunity, 1.2 million, 20 percent of the total, switched. Those who changed were disproportionately women and over age forty. This pattern was the same in Connecticut and Chile, where both groups were also being disproportionately concerned and worried about their retirement prospects under the private plans.

In 2008, after the window closed, the recession hit full force and those still in the AFJPs saw their accounts begin to sink dramatically. Then in October, the government intervened decisively, introducing a measure to pass the remainder of the AFJPs to the public system. The measure passed the Congress overwhelmingly, and Argentina became the first country to completely reverse a social security privatization by essentially nationalizing the system. The government justified its action as being made to protect AFJP participants whose accounts were dramatically shrinking and free up the funds to be used for more socially productive purposes, including countering the impacts of the economic recession. AFJP participants who switched over would receive the same guaranteed pensions as those who had been in the public system their entire work lives. What they lost by joining the AFJP system was restored.

As can be imagined, reactions to the nationalizations varied widely, from strong support to strong opposition. The AFJPs organized a protest demonstration that drew thousands. Most of the international financial press condemned the action and suggested darkly that government corruption was at its root. *Le Monde Diplomatique* published an article from Manuel Riesco, the Chilean CENDA researcher, that applauded the action and suggested that other countries with privatized systems follow suit. It ended with "millions of retired people from Latin America and other regions will without doubt breathe a little easier."[30]

Regardless of the goal of the action, it opened deep questions about democracy and government responsibility. It was clear that most in the AFJP wanted to remain there. For that reason, Joseph Stiglitz argued that they should be allowed to remain there.[31] On the other hand, an equally strong case could be made that the government had a responsibility to protect victims of a financial swindle, even if the victims did not know that they were victims. If, in the United States, a drug manufacturer started advertising pills to cure cancer with invented claims of high success rates, the Food and Drug Administration and other government agencies would intervene to stop the sales, even if desperate cancer sufferers were eagerly buying the pills. The Argentinean AFJPs, like much of the financial services industry, were selling products with similarly invented claims of success rates, in these cases, in terms of supposed superiority in delivering retirement income over traditional defined benefit pensions.

REVERSAL IN BOLIVIA

In December 2010, Bolivia followed the Argentinean example and became the second country to nationalize its privatized retirement system. Bolivia had established a defined benefit pension system in 1959. In the 1990s, in line with World Bank and International Monetary Fund orthodoxy, the country instituted widespread neoliberal reforms, including privatization of its retirement system in 1997. As the shortcomings of similar privatized systems were being revealed in Chile and Argentina, criticisms arose in Bolivia. The left-wing Evo Morales presidency in 2005 created an opportunity to critically examine the system. In August 2008, the Centro Obrero Boliviano, the country's largest trade union federation, called a general strike that included the demand to renationalize the retirement system in order to create a defined benefit plan. A year and a half later, the Congress passed and Evo Morales signed the bill in 2010.

As the first countries to reverse the privatizations of their national retirement systems, Argentina and Bolivia created a model for a course of action that could be followed by Chile and countries subjected to the transformations the World Bank encouraged in the 1990s. It was also an example relevant to those of us trapped in 401(k)-like plans. If the Argentineans and Bolivians could solve their retirement crises by reestablishing national defined benefit retirement systems, why couldn't Americans reestablish occupational defined benefit pension systems?

CHAPTER 7

Turmoil in the Land of Steady Habits

The land of steady habits
—Connecticut state motto

Dave Walsh, the former state president of my union, is a stocky guy in his sixties with a soft-spoken voice. The first time I had any contact with him was when he called me at home. He was in hot water and thought that I was one of the people responsible for keeping the temperature high. Several days earlier, a friend at another campus had sent me an e-mail of a complaint that members of the union had launched against Walsh. My friend asked me to forward it to union members on my campus, Eastern Connecticut State University. The complaint was that Walsh had approved a 50 percent raise in dues in violation of a strict reading of the union constitution. The dues increase had been approved by a majority of members voting in an election. The problem was that the turnout was very low, so the majority of voters did not constitute a majority of members, as stipulated by the constitution.

I was personally not opposed to the dues increase so long as the additional revenues would be used to our advantage. But I did think that a legitimate issue had been raised, so I forwarded the e-mail to other members. Walsh was now trying to put out fires, and the local union president had informed him that I was responsible for the e-mail.

He had a nice, friendly voice that inspired some confidence. I listened as he defended the dues increase. Then I broke in to say that I was not opposed, but that I was concerned about the Alternate

Retirement Program (ARP) that I and most members were in. I told him that I had run the numbers and determined that we would receive less than half the benefits of the minority of union members in the defined benefit State Employees Retirement System (SERS). I said that the union should work for a reform allowing those of us who wanted to change to SERS to be able to do so. There was silence. Then he told me to get my figures together and we would talk to Dan Livingston, the attorney who did all of the negotiating for the state employee unions.

Within a couple of weeks, Walsh and I were in Livingston's office. The walls were covered with photographs, mostly of causes that he had represented. Livingston is a second-generation union activist; his parents were union organizers. In Connecticut, where it has become a conservative sport to attack unionized state workers, he is the chief negotiator for state worker benefits. There are a dozen different state worker unions, including the American Federation of State, County, and Municipal Employees (AFSCME); the Service Employees International Union (SEIU); the American Federation of Teachers (AFT); my union, the American Association of University Professors; and several others. Each union has its own contract for wages and other particular working conditions. Health and retirement fringe benefits, however, are negotiated and held in common. We have different wage scales but the same health and retirement benefits. That's where Livingston comes in. He negotiates those common benefits for the coalition of state employee unions—the State Employees Bargaining Agent Coalition, or SEBAC, as it is always referred to. He also represents the combined unions whenever the state is trying to extract across-the-board concessions during budget crises. In these roles, Livingston is widely regarded as a tough, committed, and shrewd defender of state workers.

He had read the paper I had sent as preparation for the meeting. I had explained how our retirement system was delivering less than half the benefits of the state pension system, yet we were contributing over twice as much for it. As he talked about it, I realized that he understood the issue clearly. He asked me some questions and seemed to be testing how much I knew; my answers satisfied him. Then he acknowledged the problem but seemed uncertain about whether anything could be done. He suggested that we ask Thomas Woodruff, the head of the state's Retirement Services Division, to prepare a report on how much it would cost for individuals to buy time in the state pension system if transfers were allowed. Woodruff was assumed to be sympathetic to union issues because he had once worked for the United Mine Workers Union. The report request was communicated to Woodruff, and I assumed that we would have an answer within a month. It couldn't be that hard to prepare an estimate. Nine months after the meeting, there was still no response from Woodruff. For three months, I repeatedly pushed to get an answer from Woodruff. None ever came.

Several years later, when I spoke with a different attorney, he sagely advised me that one of my greatest obstacles would be stonewalling by state bureaucrats. They would delay their response for as long as possible in hopes that I would go away or give up. That indeed was a lesson I had learned from the experience with Woodruff.

I kept talking to colleagues about the problem but was not making progress on that front either. The subject was either too complicated to think about or so contrary to their assumptions that they didn't want to hear it. One problem was that while I knew about the problems because I had run the numbers, they didn't. Most of them believed that they were on their way to accumulating great wealth as they saw their account balances rising above the values of their houses. They had not figured out that in order to finance a decent retirement standard of living, they would need to accumulate far more wealth than they were likely to able to do, even if their balances looked like a lot now. After a couple of years, I fulfilled the stonewalling prophecy and essentially gave up.

THE JOKE THAT STARTED A MOVEMENT

Between October 9, 2007, and March 5, 2009, the Dow Jones Industrial Average sank from a high of 14,034 to 6,594. It lost over half its value and sank any expectation of retirement security for participants in 401(k)-like plans, including the ARP. It was a toboggan slide that started with most people holding on to the belief that it was only a temporary downturn reflecting normal market volatility. But after three months, when the market had lost two thousand points, most people began to realize that they were in for something more serious but still had no an inkling of how much further down it would go. The market was sinking in gradual slides and breathtaking plunges. The steepest plunge was between October 1 and 10, 2008, when it dropped from 10,831 to 8,451.

On October 10, the employees where I worked received an e-mail notice that the representative of ING, the Dutch financial giant that managed our retirement plan, would be available for counseling about our investments. As the third-party administrator, ING was also supposed to be providing advice on how to maximize our accumulations. We received those notices every three weeks like clockwork. The message from him was always the same: save more, which of course benefited ING's bottom line. Admittedly, I was feeling particularly snide that morning. I hit the "Reply to All" button on my e-mail program and asked, "Would that also include psychological counseling, given what has happened to our retirement investments with the stock market crash?"

My question set off a round of e-mail gallows humor. The response I liked the best was, "Noooo—that would be grief counseling." After the jokes and bitter comments ran their course, I responded with a note saying that the only solution to our plight rested in a reform that would allow us to transfer our dwindling accumulations to the state's traditional pension system, a system that worked. I didn't expect anything to come of that note.

This was, of course, not the first time participants in the ARP had gone through a roller-coaster plunge. After the 9/11 attacks, the market had plunged, as it had in the 1980s and many other times. We were living the psychological lifestyle of gamblers, with ups and downs, some more enervating than others. For colleagues in the traditional pension system, things were different. The market went up. The market went down. They hardly noticed or cared since that would not affect their retirement incomes. If the market went down, that was their employer's problem, not theirs.

I didn't expect that this particular stock market crash would shake my fellow ARP gamblers out of their slumber and make them pay attention, much less want to do something to change the situation. A couple of weeks after the plunge, a member of the faculty, Marcia Mc-Gowan approached me. She said she was worried about our retirement situation and that what I had written made sense. She asked if there wasn't something we could do. I told her I had tried but no one seemed to care. But, this time is different, she argued.

Maybe she was right, I thought. Maybe the crash had awakened people from their sleepwalking and they were ready to pay attention. Okay, I thought, if she's ready to move, maybe others can be persuaded. We hatched a plan. We would get a half-dozen or so senior faculty members and administrative employees to sign a letter of concern about our common retirement plan and send it via e-mail. I drafted the letter and Marcia edited it. To my surprise, we quickly found ten people to cosign it and sent it to the entire faculty and administrative staff.

The response was immediate and positive. People were concerned. We asked them to respond if they wanted to attend a meeting. There were so many positive responses that we had to schedule a larger room and hold a second meeting. The e-mail was also forwarded throughout the state bureaucracy. I then received a telephone call from Walsh, who said he was coming to the meeting; so was Woodruff, to answer our questions.

We established meeting ground rules to prevent the management official from taking over. Comments and questions after the presentation would be limited to three minutes. They would have to be made from the floor. No one would be able to take over the podium, which would remain firmly in our hands. As added insurance, we enlisted Ross Koning, a biology professor and former local union president, as sergeant at arms.

I looked out over the seventy people assembled in the auditorium, as they pored over a packet of materials given to them at the door.

Woodruff and Walsh were seated near the rear. There were faculty members but also administrative members from middle to top management; they were also participants in the ARP. This was not a traditional labor-versus-management issue because many in management were in the same situation.

I began by explaining that, even before the stock market crash, we would have received less than half in retirement benefits than our colleagues in the state pension plan. Now with the crash, we would receive even less. And for those meager benefits, we had to contribute over twice as much. Using tables and charts, I compared what a person with my salary and twenty-five years of service would receive from the traditional pension with what I would receive based on the annuity that I could afford with my accumulations in the ARP plan. It was less than half as much. Since I had no way of knowing what other people had accumulated, I had to assume that my experience was typical.

To understand how we found ourselves in this situation, I continued, we had to look at the basic differences between defined benefit and defined contribution plans. Most of the people in the audience, despite their advanced degrees in higher education, had never heard the terms "defined benefit" and "defined contribution" before.

As the sorry state of our retirement situation grew more apparent, the mood became grimmer. I could see it in their faces. At one point, I tried to lighten things up with a small joke, but they were in no mood. The conclusion was to propose that we be allowed to change retirement systems and roll over our accumulations to purchase back time.

There were several questions about details of the presentation, but no one disputed its basic thrust. Then Woodruff raised his hand. He began talking about his past working for the United Mine Workers Union.

"You're off the point," a psychology professor shouted from the back.

Woodruff, I would later learn, is a man who can easily fill up several hours talking, and he was just warming up. But he had been cut short. He defended the defined contribution approach but said that we were now in the conditions of a perfect storm. The stock market and, thus, our accumulations were down and interest rates at historical lows, meaning that annuity returns for retirement incomes would also be very low. When he finished, he stood and said he would take questions. But Koning told him to sit down instead.

The questions resumed, and none were addressed directly to Woodruff. The takeover had been blocked, and the organizing began. The whole experience must have shaken Walsh because a day later he called to say that he was proposing that SEBAC, the coalition of state employee unions, take up the issue.

We in turn launched a local campus committee, the Committee for Equity in Retirement, a name suggested by Marcia McGowan. At our first meeting, we laid out three possible paths to the reform: a lawsuit, legislative action, and filing a union grievance. We also established a steering committee and e-mail distribution list.

We sought new members. People like Rachel Siporin, an art professor, joined our reform cause. In a message, she wrote, "I am eager to participate in this important fight for equity. I see this as the biggest union issue to come along in decades—probably in the history of our union." Bill Newell, an ex-priest, who had grown up in a working-class union household and spoke fondly of that experience, also joined.

One of the reasons why our situation was stimulating resistance was because the inequity had become so transparent, with parallel defined benefit and defined contribution systems for state employees. The stock market plunge had no impact on the benefits and did not delay retirement target dates of members of the defined benefit system. For members of the defined contribution system, the negative impact was dramatic and obvious, especially for those whose depressed portfolios meant having to delay retirement for perhaps years. Our situation was similar to that in Chile, where people were retiring at the same time from both the old INP and the privatized AFP systems. They could see the dramatic inequality of benefits. Most working situations are not as transparent. If a company switches to a defined contribution plan for new employees, by the time that they retire the members of the former defined benefit plan are far removed or dead. They will not see the inequities between the systems.

The transparency of the inequity combined with the jolt delivered by the 2008 recession provided the conditions for making fellow employees receptive to the reform that we were proposing. This was counterintuitive, especially for a number of people. Because the state budget was in crisis due to a severe shortfall in tax revenues caused by the recession, they assumed that it would be a bad time to ask for such a reform. But the economic crisis, rather than making reform impossible to achieve, was facilitating it by jolting people into motion.

THE TINFOIL HANDSHAKE

Four months into our campaign, the state budget was still reeling from the impact of the Great Recession. Republican governor Jodi Rell wanted to make up the revenue shortfall with state worker concessions ranging from layoffs to wage freezes and furlough days. Livingston, the SEBAC attorney, went toe-to-toe with her representatives in what promised to be exceptionally tough negotiations.

One of the governor's proposals was for a retirement incentive program, what state workers soon called the RIP. The idea was to offer high-seniority workers in SERS three years extra credit toward their pensions to induce them to retire. They would vacate their relatively highly paid positions to be replaced by lower-paid workers or not replaced at all, thereby supposedly saving the state money. They would then start collecting pensions, but the pensions came from a separate fund that was not counted as part of the state budget, and that fund had more than enough to make the payments.

The problem with such retirement incentive programs is that by issuing unearned credits, they compromise the long-term financial sustainability of pension funds, in effect instantly adding unfunded liabilities to them. The existence of unfunded liabilities then later becomes an excuse to cynically argue that defined benefit plans are unsustainable and need to be replaced with 401(k)s. They also pit the immediate interests of workers who are approaching retirement, for whom the incentive programs are good deals, against the interests of all other workers, including future new employees, who depend on the existence of financially healthy pension plans.

Retirement incentive programs have the same effect as "spiking," the practice of artificially driving up final salaries with overtime pay or new, more highly paid positions. Both drain artificially high, financially unsupported pension payments from the funds.

The RIP was inevitable and we knew it. The problem was that there was little in it for ARP participants. During past early retirement programs, the state had thrown a sop to these workers with onetime token payments into their accounts that were nowhere near as valuable as three-years' credit toward defined benefit pensions. In the past, all of the negotiations had been essentially about SERS interests. But now ARP participants were increasingly vocal behind the scenes.

Our committee urged the SEBAC unions to insist that ARP participants be treated equally. If the SERS members were going to get unearned credits toward their pensions, the state should develop nonprofit annuities for us. The unions agreed and put forward the proposal. The governor's negotiators adamantly said no. In the end, SERS members got their three-years credit that was worth up to $150,000 each, and we were offered a token payment of $6,000 to be spread over three years. The idea of the nonprofit annuity was replaced by a plan in which ING would solicit bids for for-profit annuities. The Republican panacea of market competition would supposedly produce better terms.

When we heard of the travesty, we immediately issued a widely circulated e-mail response: "Tinfoil Handshake for ARP Members." In it, the grossly unequal treatment of SERS and ARP members was exposed. It was the first time that ARP members had had a public response to the inequities of an early retirement program.

Shortly after the RIP injustice, the Pension Rights Center in Washington, DC, referred me to Thomas Moukawsher, a top pension attorney headquartered in Hartford. Moukawsher said that ours was not an easy case, but it was not impossible. He suggested that his firm do a feasibility study for $3,000. Even if the study indicated that we didn't have a case, it was information well worth having so we could concentrate our efforts elsewhere. If it indicated that we did have a case, so much the better. The task would be to get the unions to spring for the $3,000 cost of the study. By this time, Jim LoMonaco, the statewide union president of State University Organization of Administrative Faculty (SUOAF-AFSCME), the union for administrative employees, had joined our steering committee. When I asked him if his union would give at least $1,000 of the $3,000, he said, "Absolutely. We need that information."

SELLING FANS IN A HEAT WAVE

Our committee was still a loose organization on one campus. We knew that it had to spread to other work sites. One contact led to another and to Angela Rola on the executive board of the University of Connecticut Professional Employees Association (UCPEA-AFT), the union representing administrative employees at the other major public university system in the state. She put me on the agenda for their next meeting. When I met her in her office before the meeting, she had a printed-out copy of our new website. "There's no way that I can retire with ARP. Do you really think anything can be done?" She was serious and worried.

There were thirty representatives at the meeting, including, I discovered, a former student of mine. After some initial reports, I laid out the situation. People nodded as I talked. It occurred to me from their comments afterward that individually they had all been worried about their own retirement prospects, but they did not think it was a union issue. I just had to say that it was and they immediately agreed.

"Is there an action proposal?" one representative said with a question that was really a statement. I asked for the second thousand dollars needed for Moukawsher's legal study. It was approved immediately and unanimously. This was like selling fans in a heat wave, I thought as I left the meeting.

I think the quick unconditional support of UCPEA resulted from it being a union in which women predominated. Female administrative employees were more grounded in understanding the importance of this bread-and-butter issue. Male faculty members still had their heads in the air (somewhere else, someone remarked.) Later, when the e-mail distribution list was in the hundreds, we found that women were more likely than men to join across the board. That has also been the experience in Chile, Manuel Riesco told me.

Deena Steinberg, an UCPEA member I met later, had come across our website and sent me a long e-mail on what she knew about the deficiencies of ARP. I suggested that we meet. She arrived at the Starbucks with a sheaf of papers from her investigations. We took a large table so that we could spread them out. I had my own research for comparison. She was about my age and had worked for the state since the 1980s like me. I didn't realize that she had been engaged in a parallel campaign and, like me, no one had listened. She had arrived at the same conclusion that I had: the ARP system was hopeless. "They ought to rename it the Connecticut Retirement Alternative Program," she said. "The acronym would be more appropriate."

I spent a lot of time over the next three months during off-hours in Starbucks and in extended e-mail exchanges and telephone conversations, trying to enlist other state workers beyond our small campus to be activists in the cause. It was hard enough to get people to understand why they were being shortchanged by ARP. It was even harder to get them to try to do something about it, but it was paying off. A core of contacts, like Steinberg, was emerging around the state.

To get the final thousand dollars for the legal study, I addressed the state council of my own union. I started by asking how many of the twenty people in the room were in the ARP. All the hands went up. By this time, I had honed my presentation of the severe inequities between ARP and SERS. Because I didn't know how much each person had accumulated in his or her own ARP accounts, I developed a table that showed the astronomical and unrealistic amounts that needed to accumulate to approximate SERS pensions.

I could see the color draining from the faces of the state council members as I presented the bad news. Despite their high elected positions, they had never examined their own retirement program, much less, like the UCPEA elected board members, considered it as an issue for union redress. They approved the thousand-dollar request unanimously.

Several weeks later Walsh invited me to present the problem at a meeting in the comptroller's office where the Retirement Services Division is housed. Invitations had been sent to the state worker unions that had ARP participants. The comptroller, deputy comptroller, and Woodruff were to take part. This was to be an exchange of views on what to do about ARP.

"How long do I have for my presentation?" I asked Walsh.

"Five minutes, but no one will object if you go over a little, to maybe eight minutes," he replied.

I thought to myself, That's too short. This is a complex issue to explain. I prepared a written statement and rehearsed it to make sure that it was within the allotted time.

Twenty-five people showed up for the meeting in downtown Hartford, including several union officials I had not yet met. There was a contingent from UCPEA, none of whom I had met before. But there was no comptroller or deputy comptroller, just Woodruff.

I began with my five-minute presentation of the problem. I distributed written copies of what I had said. Then Woodruff talked about his personal history with the United Mine Workers, how ARP had developed, and how the problems would be resolved once the market recovered. After an hour, I passed a note to the moderator asking if Woodruff was going to have the floor for the whole rest of the meeting. He shook his head no. But in fact he did have the floor for the rest of the meeting. He was allowed to hold forth for an hour and fifty-five minutes. I had been given five minutes.

BACKGROUND CHECK

It was time to ask a few questions about Thomas Woodruff, the state official who kept trotting out to counter our arguments. He had managed an ING transition from TIAA-CREF, the former administrators of ARP, within two years of accepting an appointment with the State of Connecticut as director of the Retirement Services Division. The ostensible motive was to save money in administration fees. The rumored motive was to keep ING from following through on a threat to move an administrative office, along with jobs, out of state. Was there perhaps more to it?

A Google search indicated that in addition to his public position with the state, Woodruff was serving on the board of directors of an ING research institute with Ted Benna, "the father of the 401(k)."[1] When I disclosed this damning fact by e-mail to our steering committee, the pithiest response was "gad."

A few weeks later, Walsh and I were summoned to Dan Livingston's office. He advised me to be careful with the e-mail distribution list. "Assume that management is reading it," he said. At this point, there were just over one hundred on the list.

Until then, we had largely kept the discovery of Woodruff's hidden ING identity to ourselves. But the exposure was selectively disclosed to union allies. Now was such a time. I casually mentioned to Livingston that Woodruff sat on an ING board of directors. Livingston is no one's fool. His friends and enemies alike comment on how smart he is. If you're talking to him, he not only follows what you're saying but is thinking two steps ahead so is never taken by surprise. He looked up suddenly. It's the only time I've ever seen him blindsided.

Nine months after its formation, the Committee for Equity in Retirement outgrew our local campus and became a statewide organization, changing its name to the Connecticut Committee for Equity in Retirement. It was time to take the show on the road, which meant organizing ARP crisis forums around the state.

We had picked up about twenty e-mail contacts off campus. A note went out to them urging that they organize forums on their campuses to which I would make presentations. The first drew forty people. It had been preceded by considerable e-mail discussion. I gave what was becoming my stock presentation. LoMonaco joined me for the Q&A, as he would in several subsequent forums. We made a good team. I spoke about problems of defined contribution plans like ARP and what had been done in other states with similar systems and problems. He spoke about the strategy and practical realities of getting the reform to allow us to change systems.

At each forum, we harvested e-mail addresses. Within six months, the list grew from fifty to over five hundred. A number of people started their own sublists of friends to whom they regularly forwarded my e-mails. The size of the ultimate circulation was difficult to determine.

The largest forum was at the University of Connecticut. Held coincidentally on my sixty-fifth birthday, the date worked well into the presentation because sixty-five is a normal retirement age and because our system was a failure, I could not retire.

There were a dozen such forums with audiences ranging from six to over two hundred. The Industrial Workers of the World (IWW) had a slogan: to fan the flames of discontent. We were doing some serious fanning of discontent with the retirement system.

GRIEVANCE!

A year later, SEBAC, the coalition of state employee unions with Livingston as its negotiator, responded to our campaign by launching a grievance on behalf of ARP participants. The essence of the grievance was that the state had steered individuals into choosing ARP over SERS, which was a violation of the collective bargaining agreement. Universities and colleges had a particular motive in steering their employees into ARP because of the cockamamie way the state budgeted retirement contributions. It was setting aside a full 40 percent of salary for SERS participants versus only 10 percent for ARP participants, making the total compensation package for SERS participants much higher and a budget buster for universities and colleges. Universities and colleges thus had a clear motive to steer new employees into ARP.

The much lower employer contribution necessary for ARP, though, was not because ARP was inherently less expensive than SERS. It was rather because the state was merging the unfunded liability from past underfunding of SERS with its normal cost and then spreading the whole cost among SERS participants. The normal cost of SERS was actually less than that of ARP.

The grievance remedy sought was to give ARP participants the option of transferring to SERS and rolling over funds for service credits, that is, credit for years worked—exactly what we were asking for. I was in the Czech Republic for a conference when I received the news via e-mail that SEBAC had filed the grievance. I immediately forwarded it to our distribution list. The response was explosive. People were ecstatic. Something serious was finally happening.

Steering committee member Stephen Adair and I were having breakfast in a Hartford café in early 2010 with William Cibes, a former secretary of Connecticut's Office of Policy and Management, who had considerable prestige among state policymakers. We had been advised to seek him out about the retirement reform. "If you can convince Cibes, you will have a powerful ally," we had been told by a lobbyist. "If you can't convince him, I doubt that you will be able to convince anyone."

Cibes said that he had been developing a folder of ideas for how the state could reorganize to save money during the fiscal crisis. Adair and I then made the case. Allowing us to transfer retirement systems would be in the interests of the state and taxpayers for four reasons: (1) it would allow ARP members to retire and vacate relatively high-paid positions, thereby saving the state money; (2) it would bring an infusion of funds into SERS, thereby lowering the percentage of its unfunded liability; (3) the state would save money on its retirement contributions, since the normal cost of SERS to the state is lower than that of ARP, despite widespread erroneous opinions to the contrary; (4) state employees would be able to retire with greater financial security and resources, and therefore contribute greater tax revenue to the state as well as the Connecticut economy generally.

Cibes listened carefully and asked good questions, but he was not convinced that the SERS system was less expensive than the ARP one. He promised to study it further. When I got home, I sent him some sources of information. He was very much a numbers person, and I had access to numerical calculations of the costs. We exchanged a few comments. I assumed that he remained unconvinced, but at least he wasn't convinced that we were wrong.

Three months later, an e-mail attachment from Cibes arrived. Through his own research, he had become convinced that we were right, and he had written a position paper, "Should the State Change to a Defined Contribution Pension System?" to bolster the argument. The paper was directed against those who wanted to close out SERS and push all new employees into ARP in order to save the state money. It was fully consistent with our analysis. In a summary paragraph, he wrote:

> Changing the state pension system to a defined contribution plan for future employees would not save the state money. Under any scenario, the state remains liable for the amortization payments for past service liability, at 15% of payroll and growing. But right now—indeed, since 1997—all new state employees are in the Tier IIA defined benefit system, which currently costs the state less than 5% of payroll. On the other hand, a defined contribution plan, such as the Alternative Retirement Plan currently in place for higher education employees, would require a contribution from the state of 8% of payroll (AND, I observe parenthetically, would at that level produce LOWER pension benefits than the SERS defined benefit Tier IIA plan). So the choice for the future is between a cost of 15% + 5% (amortization of unfunded liabilities + full funding of the normal cost of the existing Tier IIA defined benefit plan), and a cost of 15% + 8% (amortization of unfunded liabilities + funding a defined contribution plan). To me, the choice is clear.
>
> The call to move to a defined contribution plan is very misguided.[2]

We now had high-level verification of our analysis. Our reform would be a win-win proposition for the state and us, a loss only to ING and the financial services industry. That alone, of course, would not ensure its adoption. There was still the deep and widespread public perception that public employee pensions were more expensive than 401(k)s, and ING had its own powerful allies in the statehouse who would fight to control our retirement savings.

The goal was to get the state to allow us to transfer to SERS and then purchase years of credit within it. For those approaching retirement age with many years of work, it would do little good to just be in the pension system for the time going forward. Money accumulated in ARP would have to be rolled over to SERS to purchase service credits, a straightforward trustee-to-trustee transfer of the funds. But how much would it cost to purchase the service credits? This was the key question on everyone's mind. Would people have enough in the accounts? How would that cost be calculated?

In the spring of 2010, three unions commissioned a report from Cavanaugh Macdonald Consulting, a national actuarial firm that worked for the state. The results of the study proved to be positive and promising. If the buy-in went through, while it would not be an equitable remedy to the ARP crisis, it would still be a good deal for us. We still would be paying much more for the same benefits than SERS members, but it would nevertheless leave us with much more retirement security than we had. The results confirmed that the resulting SERS pensions would be much greater than commercial annuities that could be purchased for the same amount of ARP accumulations.

THE STATE IS LEGALLY LIABLE

Angela Rola, Jim LoMonaco, and I were sitting in the high-rent offices of Moukawsher & Walsh. We had been summoned to hear the results of the legal study. I was ready for anything Moukawsher might say. If he said that we didn't have a legal case, it wouldn't be a crushing blow. We would just stop pursuing that angle and concentrate on the grievance and legislative angles. After a little small talk, he got down to business. He became a legal machine, expressing rapidly and clearly the essence of our complaint and what the legal ramifications were.

Moukawsher concluded the state was guilty of wrongdoing by not providing ARP members with adequate information. Their officials had not told new employees that the ARP and SERS plans rendered unequal benefits. Nor had they told new employees that their decisions would be irrevocable. The wrongdoing was illegal because the Retirement Commission had a fiduciary responsibility to provide the information. A fiduciary responsibility is the highest standard under the law. It serves to make the assumed trustworthiness of an agency legally binding. That fiduciary responsibility had been breached, and we could sue. It would not be an easy suit to win, but it was a suit that the courts would consider to be serious, certainly not frivolous. It would take many years to be settled and would cost in the neighborhood of $100,000.

We now had the legal information we needed. The state was legally vulnerable. We, in short, had a case. While $100,000 would be a great deal of money for an individual to amass, several unions that had legal defense funds could easily afford it. What more appropriate way would there be to invest our dues than to try to win a settlement that would greatly enhance the retirement security of significant numbers of members? On the other hand, the lawsuit would be a last resort if other remedies failed. No one relished the idea of having to wait many years for a settlement. That would delay people's retirement, and some claimants would undoubtedly die during that time.

THE ARBITER RULES

Just short of two years after the reform campaign began, I learned indirectly that the state was ready to settle with us. Then I received an e-mail from, of all people, a financial consultant: "I just heard of the settlement. Do you have any details?" It was followed by a link. It led me to the site of the University Health Professionals, the union for employees at the University of Connecticut Health Center/John Dempsey Hospital where there was another link: Award for ARP and Pension Irrevocability. I began reading, fearing that I was in store for a huge disappointment. Then I came to the words I was hoping for: "between the date of this award and December 31, 2010, all ARP members shall be given the one time opportunity to make their irrevocable choice to either remain in ARP or transfer to SERS."

I immediately forwarded the link to the steering committee. In the subject line, I wrote, "I think we won!" Just to make sure, I called Livingston, who confirmed the news.

I felt an enormous sense of relief. All my anxiety about how I and my family would fare financially in retirement suddenly lifted. The activist part of me felt an adrenalin rush. We had beat all the odds and were suddenly standing in the victory circle.

I was asked by Walsh to delay sending out the announcement to our distribution list until Livingston prepared a list of questions and answers to accompany it. I agreed, but then individual SEBAC unions began breaking the agreement. I walked around my campus and individually told our supporters. "For sure?" one said. "For sure," I replied.

When the questions and answers were ready, I sent out the news to the more than five hundred members on the distribution list. The responses flooded in, filled with gratitude and questions. Over the next two days, I answered 120 e-mail questions as best I could. On the day of the announcement, our website received 516 hits, the largest ever.

I had been telling people that I had no personal stake in how many people actually transferred. That would be their business. We had fought just to give them the right to choose, but that had been before we actually had the right to transfer. Now I was beginning to wonder. Would people know that the opportunity existed? Would people know how important it was? Would they know enough to exercise an informed choice? Did we now have further responsibilities to educate them?

The SEBAC unions initially took the position that they were not going to advise their members. Instead, they would tell them that they should consult financial advisers. That immediately sent up a red flag. Most financial advisers have a personal interest in people remaining in 401(k)-like plans such as ARP so that they can continue selling them investment advice and products. Not only was advising members to seek out financial consultants an abdication of union responsibility—a cop-out—it was potentially setting them up for harmful advice.

Then I thought about the West Virginia schoolteachers. In 1991, the State of West Virginia, in reaction to reports that its teachers' pension plan was underfunded, closed the plan to new employees and required them to enroll in a newly created, defined contribution plan. For the new plan, the state would contribute 7.5 percent of salary, and employees a minimum 4.5 percent with voluntary higher contributions. As in Chile and other similar situations, existing members of the pension plan could remain or switch to the new defined contribution plan. The Variable Annuity Life Insurance Company (VALIC), a division of American International Group (AIG), sent salespeople, including former educators, into the schools to sell their plans with overly optimistic estimations of future benefits. "They sent people to the schools to talk about your options, and it was sold very well," said Greg Merrit, a teacher with twenty-four years of experience.[3] As in the United Kingdom "mis-selling" scandal, VALIC salespeople convinced many to abandon their defined benefit pension plans, where they would have been much better off.

By 2005, it was clear that virtually no one in the defined contribution plan was accumulating enough to adequately finance retirement. The average accumulation was only $41,478. Of those over age sixty, only 105 of 1,767 had balances over $100,000.[4] A $100,000 balance, it should be remembered, would be sufficient for an annual annuity income with COLA of only $4,900 for females and $5,600 for males.

That year, West Virginia officials closed the defined contribution plan to new employees and reopened participation in the traditional pension plan for them. Meanwhile, existing teachers and other school employees in the defined contribution plan through the American Federation of Teachers and the West Virginia School Service Personnel Association began a successful lobbying campaign in the state legislature to allow them to switch to the defined benefit pension. Aside from the fairness issue, a convincing argument for legislators was that without adequate pensions, these retiring school employees would have to turn to public assistance programs that would be expensive for the state.

In 2008, the school employees were given a five-week window of opportunity to switch to the defined contribution pension program by rolling over their defined benefit accumulations into it. Seventy-eight percent did so. The conditions of the transfer were that the funds switched from their defined contribution accounts would earn them three-quarters credit in the pension system because their employee contributions of 4.5 percent had been three-quarters of the 6 percent contributions required of the pension participants. Teachers with twenty-four years of service, for example, would receive credit for eighteen years in the calculation of the pension amount after retirement. They could purchase the remaining 25 percent to bring them up to full credit by paying an amount that was 1.5 percent of the total earnings for the years being purchased plus 4 percent compounded interest. Loans paid back with payroll deductions were available to pay the extra amount. They could also use IRA or other funds that they had.[5]

Based on press accounts, I had assumed that so many transferred simply because they were aware of the dramatic benefit differences. The West Virginia teachers and other public school employees were able to see clearly the inferiority of the defined contribution approach because they had colleagues who were in the traditional defined benefit pension. They could compare retirement income prospects in hallways and lunchrooms. When they talked among themselves, they realized that none of them were accumulating enough. Some of the commentary on the case missed this point by emphasizing that their accumulations had been low because of poor investment decisions, in effect, blaming the victim. But if none of them were accumulating enough, there was no other valid conclusion to make than that it was impossible to accumulate enough, no matter how skillful or experienced the investor was. Working together with participants in a pension plan that worked also gave them an available remedy: transferring to that plan. They were able to do it equitably: they paid back to the state what it had it had given them as a retirement benefit in return for being transferred to the better plan.

Now we were in a similar situation, and I couldn't be confident that all of the potential beneficiaries of transferring knew what was going on or what they should do. I called Josh Sword, the political director of the West Virginia American Federation of Teachers, who along with the National Education Association had been responsible for winning the right to transfer. He quickly disabused me of any notion that the three-quarter transfer rate was simply because the teachers already knew what to do. As in Connecticut, there was a prescient minority who had figured it out, but most were not adequately prepared to make a choice that would have such an impact on their financial futures. "We viewed it as their last chance to retire in dignity and we had a moral obligation to educate and make them as aware of this as possible," Sword said. "We did not cross the line of telling them what to do. But we made them aware of the consequences." He and others traveled extensively throughout the state educating union members about the retirement systems.

In Argentina in 2007 when there had been a similar window of opportunity, there had been no education campaign, and only 20 percent had transferred, unlike in West Virginia, where there had been an extensive education campaign and over 75 percent had transferred. In Connecticut, we were probably closer to the 20 percent outcome if we did nothing further. We had three short months to act.

SEBAC quickly reversed course and began an extensive education campaign. Livingston traveled to campuses and other workplaces to explain the differences between the retirement systems and the nature of the transfer opportunity. Digital technology enabled disseminating the information further through online recordings of events that people could listen to or watch at home. E-mail questions kept pouring in to me, which I answered to the best of my knowledge. The distribution list took another spurt in growth, and website hits quadrupled.

While there was a core of ARP members who had been following the developments closely and were ready to transfer at the first opportunity, the majority did not know enough to make a confident choice. That it was a short period with a quickly approaching deadline produced a pressure-cooker atmosphere.

I also realized that many people were completely averse to understanding the differences between the plans. The more the differences were explained, the more their confusion deepened. The simple mathematical calculations that were required completely puzzled a number of people, including, to my amazement, heads of economics and science departments.

My goal was to enable people to understand the differences between the systems so that they could make informed choices. I began to doubt whether that would be entirely possible. There would be many people who would never completely understand and, instead, base their decisions on what others they knew and trusted did. But it was precisely people making choices based on what other people had done that had caused much of the mess in the first place.

It reminded me of why and how CENDA in Chile is involved in public education as well as social research. It is continually looking for ways to present research in accessible ways. Manuel Riesco explained how CENDA used an extraordinary example of the inequity between the two retirement systems for making the points accessible: Two women who were twins both received a science education and went to work in similar positions with the same pay. They worked for the same number of years before retiring and their starting and ending salaries were the same. Both started in the defined benefit INP system. In 1982, when there was pressure to change to the new privatized AFP system, one chose to and the other didn't. The one who stayed in the INP system has a pension that is four times higher than the one in the AFP system.

Riesco also showed me material used to educate the public, including a detailed, four-page leaflet distributed in the tens of thousands at entrances to the metro stations. Titled "Dignified Pensions Now!," it begins, "we cannot permit the playing of roulette with the retirement of Chileans. No to the institutionalized AFP robbery!" There was a graphic of a roulette table. On the third page was a table very much like the one we used in our educational materials in Connecticut.

It's difficult and confusing to show people how they are unlikely to achieve enough accumulations in a 401(k)-type contribution plan to match what they would receive if they were in the state's defined benefit pension plan. Since everyone's accumulations were different, depending on the fate of their investments, I couldn't, for example, show what a typical accumulation would be worth because there was no typical accumulation. It was easy, on the other hand, to predict what members of the defined benefit plan would receive just by knowing what their final salaries and numbers of years of service were. Not so, though, for the defined contribution plan members, all of whom had different accumulation amounts. I listed typical final salaries and what benefits they would yield in defined benefit pensions. Then I listed how much was necessary in the defined contribution plan to equal those benefits. When I distributed that table at public meetings, people gasped. They had nowhere near the amount of accumulations necessary to match the defined benefit pension benefits.

By the time I visited Chile, Riesco and his colleagues had independently come to the same solution (see tables 7.1 and 7.2). They listed benefit amounts and the accumulations needed to obtain them. They took it a step further by showing the discrimination against women inherent in any defined contribution system that calculates benefit amounts according to actuarially determined estimates of longevity, because women live longer, on average, than men. In the defined contribution actuarial world, that means that because women will be collecting pensions for a longer time than men, in order to equalize the total amounts paid out, each pension payment must be less. It makes perfect actuarial sense, but it is total human and social nonsense because women's monthly living expenses would not be lower than those of men.

In the end, I realized that all we could do was to increase the proportion of people who would be able to make informed choices as high as possible. The higher the proportion of people who knew what they

TABLE 7.1

Differences in Overall Amounts of Pensions (converted to US$)

Accumulation Needed	Monthly Pension	
	Women	Men
$20,000	$90	$104
$50,000	$220	$264
$100,000	$444	$526
$200,000	$890	$1,046

Source: Leaflet distributed by Centro de Estudios Nacionales de Desarrollo Alternativo (CENDA), Chile.

TABLE 7.2

Defined Contributions Accumulations Needed to Match Defined Benefit Pensions at Different Final Salary Levels*

Final Income	Monthly Pension with COLA	Needed Accumulation for Equivalent Annuity Income with COLA
$30,000	$831	$199,500
$40,000	$1,108	$266,000
$50,000	$1,385	$332,500
$60,000	$1,749	$419,760
$70,000	$2,160	$518,500
$80,000	$2,542	$610,000
$90,000	$2,923	$701,500
$100,000	$3,304	$793,000
$125,000	$4,457	$1,021,760
$150,000	$5,210	$1,245,000

*Assumes twenty-five years of state service; retirement in 2008 under State Employees Retirement System, Tier IIA; 5 percent annuity that includes cost-of-living adjustment.

Source: Connecticut Committee for Equity in Retirement.

were doing, the higher the proportion of people who would follow them and make the right choice. I had no doubt that it was in almost everyone's interest to transfer to SERS, even if they didn't know why.

JUSTICE DELAYED

We had won, *or so we thought.* According to the grievance award, issued in late September 2010, all transfers between ARP and SERS were to be accomplished by December 31 of that year. In October, the Retirement Commission hired tax attorneys to investigate what types of funds—such as 403(b)s, IRAs, or personal savings—could be used to purchase back time, that is, service credits, in SERS, or so we were told. On November 1, the state comptroller's office was supposed to begin transferring those who wished to change retirement systems. That date came and went with no procedure in place. The problem supposedly was that the Internal Revenue Service had not yet responded about the funds that could be used to purchase service credits. The December 31 deadline itself came and went without the comptroller's office transferring anyone.

In early January, Livingston called to tell me there had been an unforeseen problem. The tax attorneys hired by the state had said that the transfer couldn't happen until the state got a Private Letter Ruling (PLR) from the Internal Revenue Service authorizing it. Otherwise, there could be huge negative tax consequences. This could take up to two years. (I later learned that there were requests from other states for PLRs on this issue that still hadn't been answered after seven years.) I asked Livingston whether he agreed with the tax attorneys, and he said that they were only supposed to get information on what funds could be used to pay for service credits. They weren't supposed to investigate whether a PLR was necessary. Apparently, the tax attorneys and had answered a question they weren't asked and didn't answer the question they were asked. Then Livingston gave me the worst news: the Retirement Commission had voted to stop the transfer until the PLR was issued, and we had no choice but to go along with it.

Flags immediately went up. I knew that at least four states—West Virginia, Ohio, South Carolina, and Florida—had allowed such transfers. I called Josh Sword and asked whether a PLR had been required when the West Virginia schoolteachers made their transfer. "No," he said. "It sounds like someone is trying to stop you."

I had never heard of a PLR before. The idea behind it is that if people or organizations, such as the State of Connecticut in our case, want to do something that may have tax consequences but are not sure what those consequences will be, as a precaution they can have the IRS examine the question and give guidance before they take the action. The tax attorneys had stated that it was possible that there *could* be substantial tax penalties for allowing the transfer. But *could* is a word with infinite latitude from probable to remote.

It did not make sense to me that there was any probable danger of tax penalties. The transfers would be from one pretax retirement account to another. They would benefit the IRS because it would receive more revenue from the higher-income SERS pensions than the lower-income ARP commercial annuities. That other states had allowed similar transfers without seeing the necessity of requesting PLRs made it all the more suspicious that the request was a delaying tactic. At the least, the attorneys were advocating an excess of precaution.

I saw it as comparable to when people consult tax attorneys about whether to take particular deductions about which IRS rules are ambiguous, vague, or nonexistent. Most tax attorneys will advise them to take the deductions but be ready to defend them if challenged. I thought the State of Connecticut should do the same: make the transfers between ARP and SERS and then be prepared to defend them in the unlikely event the IRS decided to challenge them.

I was impatient. The two-year or more delay would cause a lot of harm. There were people who, for age or health reasons, could not afford to wait that long for this issue to be resolved. Some people on our distribution list were well into their seventies. One had deteriorating Parkinson's disease and could afford to retire under SERS but not ARP.

Every delay in implementation of the grievance award allowed ING to keep collecting its third-party administrator fees for overseeing $1.6 billion in assets, which were worth about $1.6 million dollars a year.[6]

Was it possible that there was more to the attorneys' advice than excessive precaution, which the Retirement Commission seemed to accept at face value? A quick search on the Internet revealed that the legal firm, Robinson & Cole, by its own advertising, represented "management only in all aspects of labor relations." For experience, it boasted of many victories over unions, including prevailing in a grievance contesting "the termination of a thirty-six-year employee and former local union president," "enjoining union activity through state courts," and "defeating a UNITE [union] organizing drive."[7] In addition, it had a potentially deep conflict of interest in handling the grievance award. It was a sponsor with ING and twenty-eight other financial services industry corporations of the Connecticut Insurance and Financial Services Cluster, an advocacy group "committed to strengthening and advancing Connecticut's" financial services industry.[8] It was the only legal firm that was a member of the advocacy group.

The Insurance and Financial Services Cluster had lobbied against such labor-supported legislation as a bill that would reform healthcare delivery in Connecticut by providing nonprofit health insurance and a bill that would "prohibit an employer from coercing employees into attending or participating in meetings sponsored by the employer concerning the employer's views on religious or political matters."[9] This latter bill was a key part of the national union legislative agenda because management uses such captive worker meetings to threaten workers with loss of jobs if they vote for union recognition.

The Robinson & Cole attorneys, Bruce B. Barth and Cynthia R. Christie, had coauthored an article in the *Journal of Retirement Planning* advising companies on how to reduce or eliminate entirely contributions to their employees' 401(k) retirement plans.[10] ING had an ownership share in Wolters Kluwer, the Dutch-based publisher of the journal. To make matters more infuriating, the Retirement Commission directed that the Robinson & Cole fees "be paid for out of plan assets."[11] In other words, it used our money to pay for a legal opinion that was against our interests.

Neither the text of the Robinson & Cole opinion nor the letter requesting it were released to the public, forcing our organization to file a Freedom of Information Request to obtain it. If we had paid for the Robinson & Cole opinion, it seemed logical that we at least be allowed to see it. The state administrative unit that oversaw Freedom of Information requests did not see it that way. Citing attorney-client privilege, it ruled against us; we were not allowed to see the letter.

OUT OF FINANCIAL SERFDOM—AT LAST

Meanwhile, Connecticut's first Democratic governor in twenty years took office. Immediately confronting him was a budget crisis. With the state's economy still reeling from the Great Recession, tax revenues were inadequate to maintain normal services. He demanded concessions from state workers. The negotiations with SEBAC wound on through the spring and summer, with the concessions package first rejected and then finally ratified by employees. Our committee took the position that SEBAC should leverage the concessions negotiations to win the right to transfer retirement systems. Each of our e-mail newsletters had the slogan, "No Transfer, No Concessions."

After months of closed-door negotiations, an agreement was struck between the state and SEBAC. In the midst of the givebacks was a little noted feature by the media. Livingston, SEBAC's negotiator, had created—and the state had agreed to—a new defined benefit retirement plan to which ARP members would be eligible to transfer; and, very importantly, the state had pledged not to delay implementation by requiring an unnecessary IRS preapproval as it had with the grievance award.

The plan was a hybrid because it included some defined contribution features—a lump-sum cash-out provision and limited inheritability—in what was essentially a defined benefit plan. It would cost employees 3 percent of salary more than the traditional SERS plan.[12] It was not the new ideal plan that I would have designed, but the more I examined it, the more I concluded that it was better than what we had won in the grievance award. The lump-sum cash-out provision was valuable and would allow new employees who didn't know how long they were going to work to hedge their bets. If they lost or left their jobs, they would keep their right to a pension, as with all defined benefit plans. But that would not be worth much if they left at an early age. The final salary—the key determinant of the pension size—is a lot lower at an early age than at retirement. The lump-sum cash-out provision solved that problem. The state would keep an accounting based on the employee contribution of 5 percent of salary, an employer match of 5 percent, and a guaranteed rate of 4 percent interest. The employee at retirement could then choose which was more favorable, the cash-out or the pension. The hybrid plan also had a limited inheritance provision. If retirees died before receiving as much in pension payments as they contributed, the balance would go to beneficiaries, as in defined contribution plans.

I was among the first to transfer. Nearly three and a half years after the first public meeting about the retirement crisis, I was finally in a defined benefit retirement plan. My annual retirement income would increase by $20,000. That would put me comfortably over the 70 percent of final salary that experts say is necessary for security. I—and a lot of others—would have the classic three-legged stool at last: Social Security, a defined benefit pension, and savings.

CHAPTER 8

What We Can Do

The retirement crisis is real in the United States and in many other countries subjected to the same replacements of stable defined benefit pensions with shaky 401(k)-like investment schemes. Accounts such as 401(k)s and similar plans have proved to be insufficient to provide adequate retirement security. Fortunately, most workers in the United States have Social Security as a backup that will keep them from facing poverty in their senior years. But the goal of retirement policy should not be just avoidance of poverty. It should be maintaining preretirement standards of living. Retirement should not push people off personal fiscal cliffs into much lower budgets or dependence on younger family members. The Boston College Center for Retirement Research estimates that at least 51 percent of American households, using very conservative assumptions, are at risk of being unable to maintain preretirement standards of living after retirement.[1]

Social Security was not designed to replace enough income to maintain preretirement standards of living. It was assumed that in order to maintain those standards of living, retirees would need sufficient additional income from occupational pensions. Past defined benefit pensions did provide enough supplemental income for those workers who had them, as do current defined benefit pensions for workers, including public employees, who still have them. But the wholesale conversion in the private sector from defined benefit to defined contribution plans of the past thirty years dramatically lessened seniors' ability to supplement Social Security with enough retirement income. As a result, the occupational leg of the three-legged stool of retirement income has become increasingly shorter, undermining the stability of the stool. For many, the third leg of personal savings is nonexistent.

Some would make the situation worse with what amounts to a war on the elderly. They urge reducing the benefits of Social Security and forcing more workers into defined contribution occupational accounts. The combined result is to reduce the portion of national income available to the population over age sixty-five.

The financial services industry has its own self-serving answers for the retirement crisis, once the strategy of blaming the victim for not saving or investing wisely runs its course. The industry has a series of reforms that could be adopted that would leave its basic profitability untouched and, in some cases, enhanced. In answer to the criticism that not all workers participate when 401(k) plans are available, the industry would make participation mandatory with automatic enrollment, a proposal endorsed by President Barack Obama in his 2010 State of the Union address. This, of course, would bring a bonanza of new business to the financial services industry. In answer to the criticism that most participants are not sophisticated investors, the industry would create default automatic investment patterns. Investments would be automatically diversified and rebalanced between more risky equities and less risky bonds as workers aged. In answer to the criticism that participants often withdraw retirement savings to pay for other expenses, the industry would prohibit such withdraws—an advantage for the industry since it would keep more funds under its management. In answer to the criticism that workers changing jobs often take their 401(k) funds as lump sums and spend them, the financial services industry would make rollovers into new 401(k) or IRAs automatic. In answer to the criticism that retirees who take their accumulations as lump sums run the risk of outliving their funds, the financial services industry would require automatic purchase of lifelong annuities, as is required in the United Kingdom.[2]

While those reforms, even those that directly benefit the financial services industry, would probably improve retirement income, they would not resolve the retirement crisis. There are many defined contribution plan participants who have followed all of those ideas and still have come up substantially short. They still do not have enough accumulations to replace enough of their preretirement income. The reforms taken together would, at best, change worse to bad retirement situations.

The only meaningful reforms, short of substantially increasing employer and employee contributions into defined contribution plans that would be unnecessarily expensive, are those that increase coverage and guaranteed defined retirement benefits. These include reversing privatizations of national retirement systems in those countries where that has occurred and allowing workers to transfer out of defined contribution and into defined benefit plans.

As much as defined contribution plans have replaced defined benefit ones in the private sector, it is important to remember that there is an even more serious problem. Close to half of private-sector employees have no retirement coverage at all beyond Social Security. Any comprehensive national retirement reform will have to address this lack of coverage. And, as in the case of health-care coverage, this is not an either-or question. It also depends on how adequate the coverage is. A retirement plan, like a health insurance plan, that only delivers token benefits is better than nothing but is hardly a full solution.

I'm struck by how much politicians and the media in the United States take for granted that there is no turning back in replacing traditional pensions with 401(k) accounts, even if they demonstrably don't work well for retirees. Why is there no turning back? In his 2009 State of the Union address, as 401(k) balances were in freefall, after the stock market crash, President Obama said that one of his proposals would make it easier for workers to save for retirement, meaning in defined contribution programs. The president was repeating the great myth: each worker could save enough individually for her or his retirement, despite the blatant evidence that he or she was pouring their savings, at least for the moment, down a financial rat hole. The problem, as we have abundantly seen, is that while savings can provide part of what is necessary for retirement security, personal savings alone, even if invested skillfully and in the absence of periodic stock market disasters, are insufficient to provide enough for the vast majority of people. Reliance on savings alone will only deepen the retirement crisis.

STRENGTHEN AND EXPAND SOCIAL SECURITY

The retirement crisis calls for national action. To begin, we must acknowledge what has worked. Social Security is the most successful retirement program by far in terms of the number of people who have benefited. Its basic approach—dedication to financing retirement rather than creating wealth or providing business for the financial services industry—remains sound.

Criticisms of Social Security have been based on the claim that it is going bankrupt. Even if it were true that eventually Social Security's expenses would be greater than its revenues, that problem is easily solved. As any accountant knows, there are two possible ways to balance incomes and expenses: increase revenues or decrease expenses. There is no requirement that either, or some combination of the two, be done dramatically. Slight incremental increases or decreases will have significant consequences. That is what has always been wrong with the sky-is-falling, scaremonger argument. That said, decreasing expenses should not be pursued because it would aggravate the retirement crisis. These include proposals to either increase the retirement age, which would be grossly inhumane for people with physically demanding occupations, or decrease cost-of-living adjustments.

Rather, the long-term fiscal stability of Social Security can and should be ensured by increasing revenue into the system. Social Security revenue could be significantly increased by removing the cap on wage and salary income ($113,700 in 2013) and exposing property income (capital gains, profits, rents, and so on) to taxation.[3] Removing the cap on wage income while keeping the benefits capped, according to a Congressional Research Service study, would completely eliminate the system's shortfall, produce a surplus, keep it solvent for seventy-five years, and allow it to *lower* its tax rate on income.[4] The study did not consider the impact of instituting taxation of property income, the bulk of the income of the rich. My own calculations indicate that Social Security revenue could be increased a further $91.1 billion—over half as much as the gain from removing the cap on wage income—if property as well as wage income were exposed to taxation.

If we assume the value that we are all responsible for supporting the elderly through Social Security, the rich simply do not pay their share. By my calculation, the proportion of income subject to Social Security taxation for those earning less than $100,000 a year is 79.6 percent; for those receiving more than $10 million, it is only 0.3 percent.[5] The problem of the rich not paying their share has placed a growing strain on Social Security revenue as they have increased their share of national income over the past three decades. Progressively more income is beyond the reach of Social Security taxation. In 1983, the Greenspan Commission raised the Social Security tax rate and decreased benefits so that the program would be fully solvent until at least 2060. Yet now there are shortfalls projected before then. The reason, according to Paul Krugman, is not because of increasing longevity, which was built into the commission's calculations. Rather, it is because of "rising inequality, which has led to a growing share of income coming above the payroll tax cap, so that Social Security revenue lags behind overall compensation."[6]

SUPPLEMENTARY SOCIAL SECURITY ACCOUNTS

Retirement programs tied to particular employers are increasingly irrational. At one point, employers found them advantageous because they were an incentive for employee loyalty. If employers wanted to keep long-term workforces without having to go through the expenses associated with turnovers—loss of experience, costs of training—the company pensions served as incentives for employees to stay put. But that is no longer the case as it once was. Employers today are more likely to want flexible workforces to whom they do not have long-term commitments and that they can easily acquire when needed and lay off when not. Indeed, flexibility and contingency have become watchwords of the new economy.

These are not good developments for working people. Eliminating employment security has enormous negative social consequences. Families that have to move for job-related reasons are uprooted families. Living with continual economic insecurity brings psychological stress. The stress occurs not only between times of employment, but also during employment if a worker knows that the employment may not last.

The need for pension portability reflects growing corporate freedom to move capital. Earlier, when corporations rewarded and wanted to retain valuable workers, workers had more freedom of movement than did companies. Most of the value of a company was in its physical structure, which would be prohibitively expensive to relocate. Workers could more easily move to another state than could a company. That balance has now reversed. The cost of the physical structure of a company is no longer as much an impediment to moving as it was. It no longer ties production to particular communities. Free trade agreements and improvements in transportation make it much easier for corporations to move production sites to areas with lower labor costs, taxes, and less union representation within or outside the United States. Capital's new freedom of motion has meant that there is less job security for workers. The attractiveness of the 401(k)'s portability as a false solution reflected this. Portability came with a heavy trade-off in adequacy of retirement income.

What is needed is a system in which workers can go from job to job and continue building up their retirement security. Social Security provides an ideal base because it is a national system. But now it does not provide enough income replacement to maintain preretirement standards of living. To resolve that problem, Social Security could be expanded so that employers could begin eliminating their employee retirement plans and redirecting contributions into new supplementary Social Security accounts. The accounts would increase Social Security benefits for participants. Elimination of individual company retirement plans and the simultaneous increase of Social Security contributions would provide guaranteed adequate retirement income for all participants. This would be a fully portable public option to the current private plans.

At first, only a few companies would take part. New employees would be told that their retirement plan was enhanced Social Security participation. If they left that job and went to another employer that did not participate in the enhanced system, they would still have credit in the system that would pay off at the time of retirement. As more companies joined the enhanced system, mobile workers would build up more credits within it.

Currently, many companies don't like defined benefit systems because they have to assume all of the risks of pension fund investments. Defined contribution systems are attractive to them because once they make their payments, they have no further responsibilities. That advantage for employers would carry over to an enhanced Social Security system. Just as with the current defined contribution plans, once employers have made their contributions, they would have no further responsibility for the solvency of the fund and its future obligations to participants.

In addition to employment-based, supplementary Social Security accounts, there should also be an option to allow the establishment of supplementary IRAs within Social Security. Essentially, Social Security would be expanded for the active workforce so that it would have basic and supplementary components. Basic Social Security would be the current system that covers 94 percent of the workforce. Supplementary Social Security would comprise the additional employment-based and individual accounts. Supplemental Social Security would be available to replace—or in most cases, *add*—the second and third legs of the stool.

To understand how employment-based and individual supplementary accounts could work, we need to look at how Social Security currently calculates benefits. It determines them by averaging the thirty-five highest-earning years with compensations for the effects of inflation. Basing the formula on the average of the thirty-five high-est years rather than the final year, as do many other defined benefit pensions, avoids the problem of spiking—artificially increasing final salaries and thus pension payments through excess overtime and other means, which places loads on defined benefit pension funds that cal-culate benefits in that manner. The Social Security cap on income taxed also results in a cap on benefits that can be received. That is currently $40,200, or 25 percent above the median national income for individuals.[7] (The reforms that I am suggesting would remove the cap on income taxed but maintain it on maximum benefits.)

Few people pay the maximum amount of taxes into the system at the beginning of their working years. Thus, few workers, even if they contribute the maximum amounts in their final working years, will achieve Social Security's highest possible benefit. The supplementary accounts would allow the supplementary taxes to be applied to the years of less-than-maximum contributions and thus increase the retire-ment benefits. Individuals who maximized their basic Social Security benefits in that way and still had funds left over would automatically have the excess funds applied to life annuities upon retirement.

SOCIAL SECURITY ANNUITIES

Any national plan to resolve the retirement crisis will have to provide relief for those who currently have the bulk of their savings in defined contribution plans. The quickest way to provide relief is to make avail-able nonprofit annuities. Right now, the financial services industry extracts defined contributions from plan participants the maximum of profits in both accumulation and spend-down phases of their retire-ment plans. For the accumulation phases, regulations to control open and hidden fees will provide modest gains for participants. Far more relief can be obtained from the spend-down phase.

Any comprehensive national retirement reform should be built on the premise that the bulk of retirement income will be guaranteed for the remainder of life. The current private account system, which allows people to continue gambling with their accounts after retirement, should be eliminated. As in the United Kingdom, it should be mandatory for retirees to transfer their accumulations into life annuities. There are many reasons why that would be good policy in the United States as well. It would eliminate the risk that people outlive their incomes. It would eliminate the risk of sharp stock market downturns reducing retirement incomes. It would also eliminate the problems of adverse selection—people who live longer than average disproportionately purchasing annuities and thereby driving up their expenses—thereby lowering the costs of annuities. In brief, it would both increase and stabilize retirement incomes.

But for annuity purchases to be mandatory, they must be at fair prices, which they currently are not. Annuities cannot provide both substantial profits to the financial services industry and adequate income for retirees. The first is at the expense of the second. For the second to be attained, the first must be eliminated. That is, at-cost nonprofit annuities must be made available for holders of current private accounts to purchase upon retirement.

There are many reasons why nonprofit annuities could pay off much better than for-profit ones. Both types of annuities are based on pooling, but nonprofit ones more so because their pools would be larger with greater socialization of risks. There are no commissions, fees, or profits in nonprofit annuities. The problem of adverse selection would be minimized because of the greater size of the pool.

One primary reason why Social Security is so successful is because it is dedicated solely to providing income for its participants. No company is raking in profits off it, and its administrative costs are minimal. That would make Social Security an ideal agency for selling at-cost annuities to retirees with private accounts. Retirees would purchase nonprofit annuities directly from Social Security rather than from for-profit insurance and other financial services companies. Retirees could gain as much as 40 percent more income from public at-cost annuities than the current commercial market ones.

Those with defined contribution and IRA accounts should be allowed to roll those funds into Social Security upon retirement to maximize their benefits, as with the proposed supplementary accounts. If there are leftover amounts in their private accounts, they should be allowed to increase their retirement incomes further by purchasing life annuities from Social Security in the same way as holders of the proposed supplementary Social Security accounts would. For an extra cost, these could include an inheritability feature for those who wanted it. That is, for those who died early before receiving all that they had invested in the annuities, the unspent balances would go to their estates. It would thus be possible to achieve a Social Security income that was in excess of its normal maximum.

Public at-cost annuities could also be sold by current state or local public employee defined benefit pension funds. That would give other employees an interest in the preservation of those funds and thereby undercut the conservative campaign to eliminate them. As in the case of Social Security, an infusion of income from annuity sales would be financially beneficial to the funds. Essentially, this would represent a nationalization of the annuity business—the creation of public options that would be so attractive that for-profit companies could not compete. It would be similar to how the federal government during the Obama administration changed the way federal student loans were administered. Instead of loaning the money to commercial banks that then loaned it to students with a substantial interest surcharge, the federal government eliminated the commercial bank intermediaries and directly loaned to students, thereby saving students the excess interest charges. The federal government would have every right to argue that since it had subsidized the accumulation phase of defined contribution accounts through their privileged tax status, it had a right to be involved in how those funds were used to finance retirement annuities during spend-down phases.[8]

In 2012, the Internal Revenue Service under the Obama administration took a step in this direction. For employers who had both defined benefit and defined contribution plans, the IRS issued new guidelines to facilitate the direct sale of annuities from the pension funds to those with defined contribution accumulations upon retirement.

TAKE CONTROL OF YOUR RETIREMENT PLAN

By taking control of your retirement plan, I don't mean becoming an expert investor of personal retirement savings in a defined contribution plan or IRA. No matter how good you get at that, it is unlikely to produce the retirement security that you need. Rather, taking control of your retirement plan means understanding what you need to achieve retirement security—at least 70 percent of preretirement income—and then doing what you can to make that happen. It will require realistically assessing the retirement plans and savings that you now have, their likely trajectory, and whether the end result will achieve security or leave you short. It may mean a decision to seek a different job with a better retirement plan or actively changing the one that you have.

The first task is to become knowledgeable about retirement planning and your own situation. Don't do as I did and wait until you are in your fifties to begin thinking about it. If you do, you will surely make mistakes that will cost you, as did I. If I had known then what I know now, I would not have made the single greatest financial mistake of my life in 1986: sleepwalking into a defined contribution plan when a far better defined benefit one was available. Even though I was able to eventually reverse that mistake through a lot of work, I was not able to recover all of the losses that it cost me. Today I would be tens of thousands of dollars ahead if I had not chosen foolishly in 1986. I had to pay 5 percent in employee contributions for twenty-five years—a total sum that is too depressing for me to want to calculate now—when my colleagues in the defined benefit plan paid nothing. Even with all those payments, there was still not enough in the defined contribution account to pay for the transfer. I had to come up with still more from other sources. It also cost me over four years of organizing work to make the transfer possible, though I am not complaining because it provided other nonfinancial rewards. It was satisfying to engage in a struggle that would benefit a lot of people, as well as myself. It also produced this book. Nevertheless, the sooner you become aware of what is at stake, the better.

As I became more knowledgeable and outraged about how the financial services industry, egged on by conservative free-market think tanks, was little by little swindling working people out of their retirement savings and endangering their security in old age, I began to think that there should be some kind of mandatory teaching about retirement planning in *high school* before people enter their second age. But what high school student would treat that subject with more than a yawn? At sixteen or seventeen, who wants to think about their financial situation a half century later? Who would determine what students should learn about retirement planning? I can imagine the financial services industry leaping at the opportunity to begin selling retirement "products" to sixteen-year-olds (and their parents) with promises of fabulous returns to come. No, the best we can do now is a guerrilla campaign of information to soberly describe the realities of retirement financing and help people avoid being swindled out of their hard-earned savings.

The message of this book for individuals worried about their own retirement security boils down to two propositions: Social Security is an excellent program that contributes significantly to retirement security that should be expanded; and defined benefit plans are better than defined contribution ones. The best situation is to have a job with both Social Security and defined benefit plan coverage. The worst is a job with no type of retirement coverage whatsoever. In between is the problematic situation of most employees and probably readers of this book: having a job with Social Security and a defined contribution plan.

MAKE SURE YOUR JOB IS COVERED BY SOCIAL SECURITY, UNLESS . . .

With 94 percent of labor force participants covered by Social Security, only a dwindling number of formal jobs are not covered. But it is not just a question of currently being covered. It is also a question of how consistent the coverage was in the past and will be in the future. In my case, I was not covered from 1986 to 1990, when I began working at my present job. I also had years of very low income. That lack of coverage and low incomes during those years reduce my retirement benefit.

There are many people who go back and forth between covered formal-economy jobs and uncovered informal ones. If you are laid off, for example, you might do odd jobs until you find a new job. My recommendation is that you should always pay Social Security taxes for odd jobs, including consulting, income for periods when you do not have a regular job from which those taxes are deducted. The investment of those taxes—12.4 percent of income—will do much more for your retirement security than immediately spending the money will get you, no matter how necessary or tempting.

Many state and local public employees, including teachers, have occupational retirement plans but do not participate in Social Security. If they have a defined benefit plan, as most do, and the plan has a high enough multiplier—at least 2 percent times years of service times final salary—lack of Social Security coverage will not undermine retirement security. However, many of those plans do not contain COLAs to ensure that retirement incomes keep up with inflation. A strategic objective of members of those plans should be to gain COLAs. A small minority of state and local employees have only a defined contribution plan with no Social Security coverage. The majority of higher-education employees in Massachusetts fall into this category. Their retirement situation is especially problematic.

The worst retirement situation is having neither Social Security nor any kind of employer-based defined benefit or contribution plan. That includes working "off the books" or "under the table." The most obvious response to that situation is to get out of it as fast as possible and into a job that has some kind of retirement benefits. You should always be thinking in terms of immediate and long-term income, take-home and retirement pay. Whatever working situation you are in, there should be some contribution from the employer or you toward providing for your eventual retirement needs. As obvious as this point may seem, many younger workers give no thought to the reality that one day they will be old and in need of retirement income.

Homemakers, mainly women, who work outside the formal economy raising children and taking care of families, present a special issue
for retirement policy. Consider a situation in which a woman has been
married for forty years and worked at raising children and taking care
of a household. During that time, no contributions have been made to
any retirement system. Then, the death of her spouse or divorce occurs
when she is in her sixties. Fortunately, anyone who has been married
for at least ten years is eligible to receive Social Security benefits based
on the spouse's contributions. Also, in most states, occupational retirement plans are considered to be communal property to be divided in
divorce settlements.

In a little less than half of private-sector positions, Social Security
contributions are made by law, but there are no other retirement benefits. It is a situation that is more likely to characterize small than large
employers. The problem for small employers is that, as with health
insurance, establishing retirement benefits carries a higher cost than
it does for larger ones. From an employee's perspective, lack of retirement benefits beyond Social Security may be a motive to search for a
position elsewhere. Employers should always consider adding retirement benefits, and not just token defined contribution plans with no
employer matches. Their primary motive should be to provide the most
efficient plan possible, one in which the investment of their and their
employees' contributions goes the furthest in providing retirement income. In that respect, there is no question that, contrary to widely
held opinion, employers should explore defined benefit plans. It would
not be practical for small employers to establish defined benefit plans
for their companies alone because the pools would be too small. But
it would be possible to join combined-employer defined benefit plans.

IF YOU HAVE A 401(K)

The next highest number of private-sector employees has Social Security and a defined contribution plan. It is also the situation of a minority of public employees, and was my situation as well. The first task of
anyone in that situation is to examine the provisions of the plan and

determine whether it realistically provides adequate retirement income when combined with projected Social Security income.

The question in this situation is what percentage of salary between employer and employee contributions must be saved in order to achieve a 70 percent replacement rate upon retirement? That is a difficult question to answer because it depends on market performance, which is unknown. Attempts to predict retirement incomes based on modeling have had to make *assumptions* about market performance that have been overly optimistic in most cases. The other approach is to look at actual experiences with the plans.

My experience gives a rough idea of what to expect. During thirty years of employer and employee contributions, I saved an average 13 percent of my salaries in those plans. The total contributions were $253,906. At age sixty-five, the resulting accumulation of $532,208 was sufficient to purchase an annuity with a cost-of-living adjustment that would have replaced 23.7 percent of my salary at the time. Another way to look at this is that for each 1 percent of salary saved in my defined contribution plans over thirty years, I achieved about 1.8 percent of salary replacement. This last number of 1.8 percent is useful because defined contribution plans have different employer and employee total contributions that vary widely. If I had been in a typical 401(k) with a total of only 5 percent of salary invested for retirement, I would have had an even smaller replacement rate of 9 percent of final salary (5 times 1.8). If I had not had Social Security, to have reached the minimum 70 percent replacement rate, I would need to have saved between my employer and my contributions a whopping 39 percent of my salaries (70 divided by 1.8).

But, fortunately, I did have Social Security. My Social Security replacement rate was 20.6 percent, based on $191,486 total contributions. The Social Security rate of return, as discussed earlier, was thus higher than that of my defined contribution plan since the total contributions were much lower ($191,486 compared to $253,906). The total between my Social Security and defined contribution plan was still a replacement of only 44.3 percent of final income at age sixty-five. To have reached the 70 percent replacement rate, I would have had to put an extra 14 percent of my salaries into retirement savings plans [such as through 403(b)s and IRAs] to supplement that 13 percent that I and my employers contributed via the defined contribution plans. That might have been possible with a lot of strain on my daily living budgets if I had done that from the beginning of my work career. But of course, even if I had been willing to do that, when I was in my twenties I didn't know about it. It's usually not until workers are in their fifties that they think about supplementing retirement savings, if they think about it at all. By that time, it's too late to catch up. What has been lost is not just the amount of extra contributions not made, but also everything that those contributions would have accumulated in interest payments and capital gains.

Unless your combined employer and employee contributions are over 27 percent of income, you will come up short. Even if they exceed 27 percent of income, which is extremely unusual, there are no guarantees, because you will bear all of the risks of investment performance. See box 8.1 for a worksheet with instructions on how to estimate calculations for your own situation.

DEFINED BENEFIT PLANS: THE GOLD STANDARD, NOT AN ANACHRONISM

Your peace of mind as well as retirement security would be much better served by being in a defined benefit plan. When I made the switch to the defined benefit plan, my combined Social Security and employment plan salary replacement jumped from 44.3 to 60.7 percent. It was still less than the 70 percent recommended rate, but it was a lot closer. I also had modest supplemental savings in a 403(b). I plan to work until I am seventy. By waiting until then to start collecting, I will significantly increase my Social Security benefit. I am confident that the savings and increased Social Security benefit will put me over the 70 percent salary-replacement goal.

If, as in my case, your employer has a defined benefit plan, you should try to get into it. If your employer does not have such a plan,

BOX 8.1

How Much Do You Need to Accumulate in an IRA, 401(k), or Other Defined Contribution Plan?

The short answer to this all-important question, according to retirement experts, is that you need an amount that, when added to Social Security income, will yield at least 70 percent of your final salary. The following worksheet is based on that assumption. For those far from retirement, it will be difficult to estimate a final salary. For those at or near retirement, it is much easier.

1. Final yearly salary _____
2. Minimum yearly retirement income needed _____ (multiply figure in step 1 by 0.7)
3. Social Security yearly income _____ (look up your estimated full retirement benefit from your Social Security statement. It is estimated as monthly income. Multiply that by 12 to get your yearly income).
4. Defined benefit pension yearly income _____
5. Defined contribution plan yearly income needed _____ (subtract 3 and 4 from 2)
6. Defined contribution plan accumulation needed*
   Female _____ (multiply figure in 5 by 20)
   Male _____ (multiply figure in 5 by 18)

Example: final income of $100,000

1. Final yearly salary: $100,000
2. Minimum yearly retirement income needed:
   $100,000 x 0.7 = $70,000
3. Social Security income: $22,776
4. Defined benefit pension yearly income: 0
5. Defined contribution plan yearly income needed:
   $70,000 − $22,776 = $47,224
6. Defined contribution plan accumulation needed:*
   Female: $47,224 x 20 = $944,480
   Male: $47,224 x 18 = $850,032

*Accumulation needed is for purchase of a full-life annuity that includes a cost-of-living adjustment at the current average rate of 4.9 percent for females and 5.6 percent for males.

you could suggest it switch to one. Admittedly, this would be difficult. But your argument is that such a switch would be in the interests of all employees, including managers. First show the superiority of a defined benefit plan for actual benefits and its lower cost in contributions. You also could try to find a new job that does have one. Your only other remedy is to pour as much of your income as possible into supplemental savings through IRAs and the like.

If you have Social Security, a defined benefit plan, and job security, and you like your job, count your lucky stars. You are set. Your job is to protect what you and your coworkers have from those who would end your defined benefit plan voluntarily by convincing you to switch to an optional defined contribution plan or involuntarily by forcing you to. In 1984, my fellow employees were given a window of opportunity to switch from a generous defined benefit plan to the defined contribution one. Many switched, believing falsely that they would do far better. This type of voluntary switch is less likely to happen now because the deficiencies of defined contribution plans have been exposed.

You should also examine the features of the defined benefit plan. A stand-alone plan (one without Social Security coverage) should have a minimal multiplier of 2 percent. If there is Social Security coverage, the multiplier should be at least 1.5 percent. Defined benefit plans also vary according to whether they contain COLAs, a valuable feature that keeps inflation from decreasing retirement income. Workers should strive to have COLAs added if they don't exist. There are two possibilities here. The first is to simply have it added while retaining the same multiplier, thereby making the plan more expensive. The second is to compensate for the cost of the addition of the COLA by reducing the size of the multiplier. Texas public employees, for example, have a defined benefit plan with a higher than average multiplier of 2.3 but no COLA. They could approach state officials to rearrange the payout of benefits so that a COLA could be added in a revenue-neutral manner. The multiplier could be lowered just enough to allow the addition of a COLA with no net increase in costs or decrease in lifetime income to retirees. It would, of course, be nicer to get the COLA with no decrease in the multiplier. But if the add-on COLA benefit is unlikely because of stiff resistance, especially in a climate of reduced state revenues and opposition to public worker benefits, attaining a COLA in return for forgoing immediate income is worth doing because it would protect retirees from the ravages of inflation.

For those fortunate enough to have both Social Security and defined benefit coverage, there is the temptation to be complacent. You are set, assuming that your defined benefit plan has more than token salary replacement. You may want to increase further your retirement security by regularly contributing to an IRA or some other tax-privileged savings vehicle. You should also learn the details of your plans. Your main task will be to make sure that your benefits remain intact. That is, make sure that your employer does not suddenly abandon your defined benefit plan for a defined contribution plan or none at all. You will also want to make sure that you are protected should your employer go out of business. Private defined benefit plans generally have that protection through the Pension Benefit Guarantee Corporation, which insures benefits. You should be aware of worst-case scenarios.

Knowing what you have in terms of your Social Security and pension benefits will make it easier to calculate the consequences should an opportunity come along to change jobs. A friend in Massachusetts is on leave from his public university to work at a private one that he likes better. It is closer to where he lives, and the working conditions and atmosphere are more to his liking. He would almost certainly stay there, except for one problem. In Massachusetts, the situation is parallel to ours in Connecticut. The public universities have defined benefit and defined contribution retirement plans. As in Connecticut, members of the defined contribution plan now realize their disadvantage and want to transfer to the defined benefit plan. If the Massachusetts educators win that struggle, as we did in Connecticut, my friend will be in a dilemma. He may want to return to his old job to take advantage of the retirement benefit, even though he likes the new one better. As it is now, the old job falls into a category just short of the worst possibility of no retirement coverage whatsoever. There is no Social Security coverage for state employees in Massachusetts, unlike Connecticut. The defined benefit pension is generous enough—it is not unrealistic to retire at 80 percent salary replacement—to compensate for the lack of Social Security coverage. But those in the defined contribution plan have only it, and its employer match is not particularly generous. A further consideration for my friend is that the new job has Social Security coverage to partially offset its disadvantageous defined contribution plan.

One of the greatest issues facing members of defined benefit pension plans in my opinion, particularly those in public ones, concerns attempts to eliminate or sharply reduce their benefits for new employees. As discussed earlier, phasing out pension plans by not offering them to new employees is a path of least resistance for employers because yet-to-be-employed workers are by definition not there to resist. The temptation is for employees vested in the pension system with security to shrug their shoulders because they will not be harmed by the change. It is undeniable that they have no personal economic interests at stake. But I would argue that they have at the least a moral obligation to stick up for the interests of future employees. They are more likely to know what is at stake. They are more likely to be economically secure. They have the ability to resist negative changes, even if they are not personally affected by them. They will benefit from the defined benefit plan. As all parents would like their children to do at least as well if not better than they do economically, workers should do their part to protect future generations from benefit cutbacks.

There are some positions that come with both defined benefit and defined contribution plans in addition to Social Security coverage. These would seem to be the ideal retirement setup, but it depends on how good the components are. The contributions and benefits of Social Security are fixed, with no way for employers to offer stronger or weaker plans. Defined benefit and defined contribution employer-based plans, on the other hand, vary greatly in their contributions and benefits. As discussed earlier, the World Bank, despite its advice to others, provides the most generous combined retirement package for its own employees that I know of: a 1 percent defined benefit plan and a defined contribution plan with a 10 percent employer contribution. The US federal government has a 1.1 percent defined benefit plan and a defined contribution plan with a 5 percent employer contribution.

UNIONS

If you examine your retirement prospects and conclude that changes are needed in the plan that you have at work, you must first get all of your facts in order. Once you have done that, you need to be able to articulate to others what is wrong with the existing plan and how a different plan would be to their benefit. You could try to make a defined contribution plan better by increasing the employer contribution, reducing management fees, or creating different investment options. As I have argued throughout the book, those will produce only marginal improvements. If you're going to put an enormous amount of effort into reforming a retirement plan, you might as well go for a significant reform. The most significant reform for most people involves getting into a defined benefit plan. I know that the general culture is shouting that defined benefit plans are no longer on the table, so don't even try. But, there are still a sizable number of defined benefit plans that are financially healthy. There are also a small and growing number of employers who are bucking the general trend by abandoning defined contribution plans for defined benefit plans. It can be done, though it won't be easy. Don't be surprised if you find that few of your colleagues understand the plan that they have or particularly care. Especially if they are young, worrying about retirement may not be a priority.

As an employee seeking a significant benefit reform, you might be able to convince those in power in the company with the sheer validity of your arguments. You can do all of the research and write about it persuasively. You *might* be successful if you do that, and it is worth a try. My experience was, though, that it didn't work. I wrote up my research and presented it to management and union officials. They all nodded and nothing happened. Only after organizing a lot of other people who demanded change did union and management officials begin to take the reform seriously.

You will need to find allies. You don't want to be a lonely Cassandra doomed to telling a truth that no one wants to listen to. You will not need many allies to get something started, but you will need some. The Connecticut struggle made a quantum leap forward when a single person, Marcia McGowan, joined forces with me. That led more people to take the issue seriously and be receptive when we approached them to form a core group.

Most organizing drives that start from scratch operate in concentric circles. At the center, there must be someone or a small group of people who are absolutely committed to the issue and can lead. The next circle is made up of active supporters who can be called upon to help from time to time. The third circle is made up of passive supporters, those who want to be kept informed via newsletters or e-mails. While they are unlikely to put formal work into the campaign, they help to spread its influence through their own informal networks of friends and acquaintances. Beyond those circles are all of the people who would potentially benefit from the reform. As the drive progresses, more people from the outside hear about it and are drawn in.

If there is a union where you work, concentrate your energy on getting it behind the reform. The union will have far more financial and political resources than you and those who want the reform will have. In theory, unions should immediately respond when workplace issues arise, such as the exposé of retirement plan inadequacy. In practice, they don't necessarily. Union officials and officers are not just waiting for members to come into their offices with plans of action. Anything new that you bring to their attention means more work when they may already be spread thin with other issues. There is also the reality that just because something is unfair doesn't mean that a union can necessarily do anything about it. The best union officials and officers will have to weigh whether they can realistically do anything. But realism in this respect is not an exact science. Most of the union people we initially approached thought that they could do nothing. Only after organizing members in their unions who demanded that something at least be attempted did they discover that they could indeed do something.

There is thus inertia to overcome in many unions to get productive help. In other words, don't take an initial *no* for a final answer.

We never could have achieved our victory without our unions' support. Our unions never would have taken on the issue and pursued it to a successful conclusion without the continual work of our committee. Unions thus are most effective when members are actively engaged within them about issues they care about. In our case, the engagement was initiated by a rank-and-file group rather than the leadership. In the end, it strengthened the union.

We were very fortunate to have been in a context where there were unions to take on the struggle. Most workers are not because of the declining percentage of union representation, especially in the private sector. Anyone who wants to reform a retirement benefit where there is no union representation may want to consider organizing one as a first step, using the retirement issue as an enticement for other workers to join. Unions themselves could offer to fight for creating defined benefit pensions as an attractive enticement to workers to vote for them in organizing drives.

A WORD TO MANAGERS

Early in our retirement reform struggle, we realized that we were not engaged in a classic labor-versus-management conflict. Our managers were as stuck in the defined contribution plan as we were. One day, after our struggle had become very public, the executive vice president for my university went out of his way to tell me, "You're doing a good thing." He had switched from the defined benefit to the defined contribution plan years earlier and now was deeply regretting it. We would have a number of discreet conversations in which he indicated that he hoped his normal adversaries, the unions, would succeed with this reform. As a top manager, he was not represented by a union, yet he was dependent on what the unions negotiated for fringe benefits.

In most working situations, managers and nonmanagerial employees have access to the same types of retirement plans. The 401(k)-type plans harm managers as well as nonmanagers. It follows that managers and nonmanagers can and should support reforms that contribute to greater retirement security for all employees. They may have different interests than nonmanagerial employees over take-home pay issues. But their interests are the same in the types of retirement plans available.

When managers realize that defined benefit plans are less expensive than defined contribution plans, contrary to widespread belief, adoption or readoption of them becomes an obvious solution that benefits all employees. As awareness grows of how low typical defined contribution plan benefits are, there is the temptation to go the route of funding them better. That is a false solution, though.

At an early stage in our struggle, a state legislator asked me how much more the state would have to contribute to the defined contribution ARP system we were in to make its benefits comparable to the defined benefit SERS system. As it was, the state and employees were contributing a combined 13 percent of salaries to the ARP system and about 10 percent to the SERS system (despite its much higher benefits). I calculated that the combined employer-employee contribution would have to go up to 29 percent, over twice as high, for the defined contribution model to render benefits equivalent to the defined benefit one.

The reason for the great difference in cost, as I've abundantly discussed in the preceding pages, is that while defined benefit plans require funding to provide for one beneficiary—the retiree—defined contribution plans require funding to provide for two beneficiaries—the retiree and the financial services industry.

What has evolved in the delivery of retirement benefits is comparable to what exists with health-care benefits. The United States has without question the most expensive health-care system in the world. Many countries deliver the same or higher-quality health care to their citizens at much lower cost. Since health insurance coverage mostly exists as an employee fringe benefit like retirement plans, managers have an interest in lowering its cost. That has given managers outside the industries that profit from the high cost of medical care an incentive to support national health-care reform. Many have been slow to do so, in part because it does not affect their own personal health-care coverage. It is different, though, with retirement plans because the existence of 401(k) plans objectively undermines their own personal retirement income prospects. Just as there is a clash between the exorbitant profitability of the "health industrial complex" that other areas of industry resent, there is a clash between the exorbitant profitability of the financial services industry and other parts of the economy.

Companies seeking to lower their health-care costs have few options beyond shifting the costs to employees or discontinuing the benefit. But with retirement plan benefits, it is different. Companies could reinstate defined benefit plans for the same or lower costs to what they are now paying into defined contribution plans. The results would benefit them and their employees. Here, far-seeing managers could play a vital role that would be in their own financial interests and greatly appreciated by other employees. From a company perspective, having a quality retirement plan would enhance employee loyalty and decrease turnover, with its associated costs.

CONCLUSION

In summary, the massive transformation of defined benefit pensions to 401(k)-like accounts since 1981 severely undermined the retirement security of tens of millions of Americans. The double premises of the transformation turned out to be false. The 401(k)-like accounts have not produced higher retirement incomes than the defined benefit pensions that they replaced. Their rate of return is less than half. Nor have they proven to be a more economical way to finance retirement security. They require twice as many contributions to achieve the same level of benefits as traditional pensions. The reasons for this great disparity are that the financial services industry drains considerable fees, commissions, and profits from the accounts; and the defined contribution approach does not have the advantages of risk pooling that the defined benefit one has.

In tandem with the expansion of 401(k) accounts has been an attempt fanned by conservative ideologists to privatize a substantial part of Social Security. Consistent with World Bank policy, they want Social Security ultimately reduced to a means-tested program for the elderly poor, with private accounts making up all other retirement provision. In that quest, the privatization and cutting back of Social Security benefits go hand in hand. Cutting back middle-class benefits undermines the middle-class political support for the program. Once that is lost, Social Security tax rates can be reduced under the argument that the middle-class taxpayers shouldn't have to pay for a program that does not benefit them; they would do better by redirecting their Social Security taxes into private accounts.

The campaign against Social Security in this country is in line, as we have seen, with privatization campaigns in other countries, an international trend that began under the guns of a Chilean military dictatorship in 1981. Privatization of national retirement systems accelerated in the early 1990s after being endorsed and promoted by the World Bank. Substantial parts of Latin America and Central and Eastern Europe have had all or significant parts of their public retirement systems privatized. Every gain in privatization swells the profits of the financial services industry at the expense of retirement security.

We need not be passive or fatalistic in the face of these policy changes, most of which were made by economic and political elites who look forward to retirement incomes and security that the rest of us cannot imagine. We can try to improve our own prospects. We can maneuver within the policies that have been established and actively resist and reverse the most noxious of them. Despite elite policymakers wanting members of the public to believe that the changes are the only ones possible, all social issues such as retirement have policy options, including whether the primary beneficiaries will be retirees or the financial services industry. By being active on retirement issues in our workplaces and communities, we have the potential to lessen and possibly reverse the damages of the great 401(k) swindle and avoid future ones.

Acknowledgments

This book was the product of research into a problem and activism to resolve it. While I had a background in policy studies to draw upon, I doubt that I would have learned as much about the subset of retirement policy, much less written a book about it, if the Connecticut reform campaign portrayed in chapter 7 had not occurred.

The entire experience of research and activism produced debts to a number of people, with there being no hard wall between the types of help. Marcia P. McGowan, Stephen Adair, Deena Steinberg, Rachel Siporin, Michael Kurland, John Briggs, Jim LoMonaco, and Anne Dawson consistently worked on the Connecticut campaign with critical ideas for strategy and honing of arguments, including on important occasions toning down my public communications.

Timothy Black, Mary Erdmans, Jerry Lembcke, Christopher Doucot, and William Major—friends and members of a writers' group—offered constructive comments on an early draft.

Ricardo Dello Buono helped me with contacts for my research in Chile. Ximena de la Barra in Chile led me to the symbolic ground zero of international resistance to privatization of retirement accounts. Manuel Riesco from Chile's Centro de Estudios Nacionales de Desarrollo Alternativo (CENDA) generously shared his vast knowledge of how the Chilean privatized system had spectacularly failed to provide retirement security, despite being considered a model of reform for the rest of the world.

Any type of project like this inevitably requires legal help. Attorneys Leon Rosenblatt and Bernard E. Jacques helped to clarify the strategy for obtaining the retirement reform when most state officials were saying that it couldn't be done. What is more, they did not charge for their advice when there was no money to pay for it. Kyle Garrett and the very valuable Pension Rights Center gave advice, including the critical referral to attorney Thomas Moukawsher, who in turn provided critical legal help.

We were very lucky to have Daniel E. Livingston as the attorney and chief negotiator for the Connecticut State Employees Bargaining Agent Coalition, which represented state employee unions. Without his skill and commitment, the reform would not have been accomplished and this book would not have been published, since no one would have wanted to read about a reform struggle that failed. Sal Luciano from the American Federation of State, County, and Municipal Employees (AFSCME) in Connecticut was also instrumental in lending his prestige and a sympathetic ear to what we were trying to accomplish.

William Cibes lent his vast policy analysis skill to confirm our contentions and then his considerable prestige among state officials to clear the way for the retirement reform we were advocating.

Of all the written materials that I consulted for this work, I found Robin Blackburn's *Banking on Death* to be especially useful, as were as his comments on our reform campaign at a 2012 panel in New York on which we served.

Diana "Donnie" McGee from the Massachusetts Teachers Association spent many hours on the phone and in person comparing and analyzing our experience with retirement reform with hers in Massachusetts, where she was leading a parallel campaign. Josh Sword from the American Federation of Teachers in West Virginia generously relayed the experiences of their retirement reform campaign and offered advice for ours.

Scott Mendel, my literary agent, had doubts about publishers being interested in this project, since most of them have 401(k) plans for their own employees. But because reading it made his "blood boil," he took a risk. Eileen Sheryl Hammer and Mimi Schroeder were early enthusiastic proponents of the project. Joanna Green, my editor at Beacon Press, immediately saw the significance of the book and became a strong advocate for it. She became convinced by and embraced the goals of the book, writing to me at an early point, "I think I'm having a similar (albeit on a smaller scale) experience as you when talking about the 401(k) crisis. There are the looks of disbelief, followed by fear, ending with anger." She poured all of her belief in the cause as well as editorial skill to make the book as effective as possible. Jane Gebhart sharpened the presentation further with expert copyediting. I have long admired Beacon Press since noting at age eighteen that it was the publisher of James Baldwin's *Notes of a Native Son*, which I was reading during breaks from a job selling ice cream bars from the back of a three-wheel motor scooter in Tulsa, Oklahoma. Its strong economic justice mission makes it the perfect press for this book.

Notes

Preface

1. College Board Advocacy and Policy Center, *Trends in College Pricing 2012* (Washington, DC: College Board, 2012), figure 5, 14.

2. US Census Bureau, CPS Population and Per Capita Money Income, 1967–2011, table P-1, http://www.census.gov/hhes/www/income/data /historical/people/.

3. Recounted on *Fresh Air*, National Public Radio, May 16, 2013. See the results of his study of 401(k) administrative fees in Robert Hiltonsmith, *The Retirement Savings Drain: Hidden & Excessive Costs of 401(k)s* (New York: Demos, 2013).

4. Calculated from tables 1.5.5, 6.4B, 6.4D, 6.16B, and 6.16D of US Department of Commerce Bureau of Economic Analysis, "National Income and Product Tables" (2010).

5. Alicia H. Munnell, Francesca Golub-Sass, and Dan Muldoon, "An Update on 401(k) Plans: Insights from the 2007 SCF," no. 9–5, 2, Center for Retirement Research, Boston College, March 2009, http://crr.bc.edu/images /stories/Brief/ib_9_5.pdf; US Department of Labor, "2010 Form 5500 Annual Reports," *Private Pension Plan Bulletin*, November 2012, table A1.

6. Aon Hewitt, "The Real Deal: 2012 Retirement Income Adequacy at Large Companies" (Lincolnshire, IL: Aon Hewitt, 2012), 6, http://www.aon .com/human-capital-consulting/thought-leadership/retirement/survey_2012 _the-real-deal.jsp.

Chapter 1

1. Felicitie C. Bell and Michael L. Miller, "Life Tables for the United States Social Security Area 1900–2100," Actuarial Study No. 120 (Washington, DC: Social Security Administration), table 10.

2. Robin Blackburn, *Banking on Death: Or, Investing in Life—the History and Future of Pensions* (London: Verso, 2002), 46.

3. Alicia H. Munnell and Annika Sundén, *Coming up Short: The Challenge of 401(K) Plans* (Washington, DC: Brookings Institution Press, 2004), 5.

4. Frances Fox Piven and Richard A. Cloward, *Regulating the Poor: The Functions of Public Welfare*, (New York: Vintage, 1971, 1993), 93.

5. Ibid., 100.

6. Geoffrey Kollmann, "Summary of Major Changes in the Social Security Cash Benefits Program: 1935–1996" (Washington, DC: Library of Congress Congressional Research Service, 1996), 2.

7. "Annual Statistical Supplement to the Social Security Bulletin, 2009" (Washington, DC: Social Security Administration, 2010), 12.

8. Alicia H. Munnell and Mauricio Soto, "Sorting out Social Security Replacement Rates," *Just the Facts on Retirement Issues*, November 2005, 2.

9. Kathleen Romig, "Social Security Reform: Possible Effects on the Elderly Poor and Mitigation Options" (Washington, DC: Library of Congress Congressional Research Service, April 1, 2008), 1.

10. Social Security Administration, *Annual Report on the Social Security Disability Insurance Program, 2011* (Washington, DC: Social Security Administration), table 3.

11. Robert L. Clark, Lee A. Craig, and Jack W. Wilson, *A History of Public Sector Pensions in the United States* (Philadelphia: University of Pennsylvania Press, 2003), 2–4.

12. Craig Copeland, "Employment-Based Retirement Plan Participation: Geographical Differences and Trends," 2010, Employment Benefit Research Institute Issue Brief No. 363, October 2011, figure 1.

13. For an extensive discussion of this corporate practice, see Ellen E. Schultz, *Retirement Heist: How Companies Plunder and Profit from the Nest Eggs of American Workers* (New York: Portfolio/Penguin, 2011).

14. US House of Representatives Ways and Means Committee, *Green Book 1998*, tables 1-2 and 1-17.

Chapter 2

1. Milton Friedman, *Capitalism and Freedom* (Chicago: University of Chicago Press, 1962), 6.

2. Louis Hartz, *The Liberal Tradition in America* (New York: Harcourt, Brace & World, 1955).

3. Seymour Martin Lipset, *American Exceptionalism: A Double-Edged Sword* (New York: W.W. Norton & Company, 1996), 36.

4. Friedman, *Capitalism and Freedom*, 35, 182–88.

5. Milton Friedman and Rose Friedman, *Free to Choose: A Personal Statement* (New York: Harcourt Brace Jovanovich, 1980), 107.

6. Naomi Klein, *The Shock Doctrine: The Rise of Disaster Capitalism* (New York: Henry Holt and Company, 2007), 62.

7. José Piñera, "How the Power of Ideas Can Transform a Country," http://www.josepinera.com.

8. US Department of Labor, "1995 Form 5500 Annual Reports," *Private Pension Plan Bulletin*, no. 8 (Spring 1999): table E8.

9. Alicia H. Munnell, Francesca Golub-Sass, and Dan Muldoon, "An Update on 401(k) Plans: Insights from the 2007 SCF," paper no. 9–5, Center for Retirement Research, Boston College, March 2009, 2, http://crr.bc.edu /images/stories/Brief/ib_9_5.pdf; US Department of Labor, "2010 Form 5500 Annual Reports," *Private Pension Plan Bulletin*, November 2012, table A.

10. Earl A. Reitan, *The Thatcher Revolution: Margaret Thatcher, John Major, Tony Blair and the Transformation of Modern Britain* (Lanham, MD: Rowman & Littlefield, 2003), 17.

11. Social Security Project, "Broken English: The United Kingdom's Troubled Experiment with Personal Pensions" (New York: The Century Foundation, 1999); Norma Cohen, "A Bloody Mess," *American Prospect*, January 11, 2005; Robin Blackburn, *Banking on Death: Or, Investing in Life—the History and Future of Pensions* (London: Verso, 2002), 287–90.

12. Rupert Jones, "Final Salary Pension Schemes 'to Be History by 2012,'" *Guardian*, August 2, 2006.

13. Teresa Ghilarducci, *Labor's Capital: The Economics and Politics of Private Pensions* (Cambridge, MA: MIT Press, 1992), 87.

14. Ellen E. Schultz, *Retirement Heist: How Companies Plunder and Profit from the Nest Eggs of American Workers* (New York: Folio/Penguin, 2011), 13.

15. Ibid., 15.

16. US Bureau of Labor Statistics, 2012 National Compensation Survey, tables 2 and 8.

17. Norma Cohen, "Pension Scheme Membership Falls," *Financial Times*, October 12, 2007.

18. Jilian Mincer, "Many U.S. Employers Cut 401(K) Matches," *Wall Street Journal*, March 26, 2009.

19. Helaine Olen, *Pound Foolish: Exposing the Dark Side of the Personal Finance Industry* (New York: Portfolio/Penguin, 2012), 82–84.

20. The College Retirement Equities Fund (CREF) was added in 1952.

21. Teachers Retirement System of Texas, *Pension Benefit Design Study*, September 1, 2012, figures 5.1 and 5.3.

Chapter 3

1. James S. Henry, "The Other September 11," *Forbes*, September 10, 2011.

2. Ibid.

3. Joseph Collins and John Lear, "Pinochet's Giveaway: Chile's Privatization Experience," *Multinational Monitor* 12, no. 5 (May 1991).

4. Orlando Caputo and Gabriela Galarce, "Chile's Neoliberal Reversion of Salvador Allende's Copper Nationalization," in *Neoliberalism's Fracture Showcase*, ed. Ximena de la Barra (Leiden, Netherlands: Brill, 2011), 47.

5. José Piñera, "Wealth through Ownership. Creating Property Rights in Chilean Mining," *Cato Journal* 24, no. 3 (Fall 2004): 299.

6. Caputo and Galarce, "Chile's Neoliberal Reversion," 61.

7. Joseph Collins and John Lear, *Chile's Free Market Miracle: A Second Look* (Oakland, CA: Food First Books, 1995), 130.

8. Marta Harnecker, "Where Was the Chile I Left Behind," *Neoliberalism's Fractured Showcase*, 93.

9. Naomi Klein, *The Shock Doctrine: The Rise of Disaster Capitalism* (New York: Henry Holt, 2007).

10. "The Pinochet Paradox," *Wall Street Journal*, December 12, 2006; Geri Smith, "Augusto Pinochet's Uncomfortable Legacy," *Business Week*, December 11, 2006; Rich Karlgaard, "Pinochet and the *New York Times*," *Forbes*, December 11, 2006.

11. "After the Coup in Cairo," *Wall Street Journal*, July 4, 2013.

12. Robert Holzmann, Richard Paul Hinz, and Mark Dorfman, "Pension Systems and Reform Conceptual Framework," *Social Protection and Labor* (Washington, DC: World Bank, 2008), 1.

13. Robin Blackburn has stressed the importance of Summers' role at the time that the World Bank was formulating its approach to retirement reform. See Robin Blackburn, *Banking on Death: Or, Investing in Life—the History and Future of Pensions* (London: Verso, 2002), 229.

14. World Bank, *Averting the Old Age Crisis: Policies to Protect the Old and Promote Growth* (New York: World Bank, 1994), 14.

15. Ibid., 15.

16. Holzmann, Hinz, and Dorfman, "Pension Systems and Reform Conceptual Framework," 6.

17. I have written about NAFTA resulting in peasant ruin and migration in *Class and Race Formation in North America* (Toronto: University of Toronto Press, 2009), chap. 7.

18. Katharina Müller, "The Making of Pension Privatization in Latin America and Eastern Europe," *Pension Reform in Europe: Process and Progress*, ed. Robert Holzmann, Mitchell Orenstein, and Michal Rutkowski (Washington, DC: World Bank, 2003), 61.

19. Jiunjen Lim, "Pension Reform in Russia and Kazakhstan," *Wharton Research Scholars Journal* (2005), http://repository.upenn.edu/wharton_research_scholars/27/.

20. Richard Disney, "Notional Defined Contribution Plans as a Pension Reform Strategy," *World Bank Pension Reform Primer* (Washington, DC: World Bank, 1999). The primer, available online and continually updated, is described as a World Bank "comprehensive, up-to-date resource for people designing and implementing pension reforms around the world."

21. Lim, "Pension Reform in Russia and Kazakhstan."

22. World Bank, "Staff Retirement Plan: Net Plan Highlights" (2010).

23. World Bank, "The World Bank Group Headquarters 401(K) Plan" (2010).

Chapter 4

1. Milton Friedman and Rose Friedman, *Free to Choose: A Personal Statement* (New York: Harcourt Brace Jovanovich, 1980), 297.

2. Peter J. Ferrara, *Social Security: The Inherent Contradiction* (San Francisco: Cato Institute, 1980), 9.

3. David A. Stockman, *The Triumph of Politics* (New York: Harper & Row, 1986), 193; cited in Robin Blackburn, *Banking on Death* (London: Verso, 2002), 359.

4. Sylvester J. Schieber and John B. Shoven, *The Real Deal: The History and Future of Social Security* (New Haven, CT: Yale University Press, 1999), 186.

5. Stuart Butler and Peter Germanis, "Achieving a 'Leninist' Strategy," *Cato Journal* 3, no. 2 (Fall 1983): 552.

6. Ibid., 547.

7. Ibid., 552.

8. Ibid., 548.

9. Calculated from Employee Benefit Research Institute, *EBRI Databook on Employee Benefits* (Washington, DC: EBRI, 2010), tables 2.1, 2.2, and 2.3; Social Security and Medicare Boards of Trustees, "A Summary of the 2010 Annual Reports," http://www.ssa.gov/OACT/TRSUM/index.html; Investment Company Institute, "The U.S. Retirement Market, First Quarter, 2010" (Washington, DC: ICI, 2010), figure 1; US Department of Labor, *Private Pension Plan Bulletin,* "Abstract of 2007 Form 5500 Annual Reports" (Washington, DC: US Department of Labor, 2010), table A4.

10. Cato Institute, *Cato Handbook for Policymakers*, 7th ed. (Washington, DC: Cato Institute, 2009), 181.

11. Ibid., 183.

12. George W. Bush, *Decision Points* (New York: Crown Publishers, 2010), 297.

13. Deputy Secretary of the Treasury Lawrence H. Summers, testimony before the Senate Finance Committee, July 22, 1998.

14. Butler and Germanis, "Achieving a 'Leninist' Strategy," 554.

15. Social Security Advisory Board, "The Social Security Statement: How It Can Be Improved" (Washington, DC: Social Security Administration, 2009), 7.

16. Michael Dolny, "What's in a Label? Right-Wing Think Tanks Are Often Quoted, Rarely Labeled Extra!" *Fairness and Accuracy in Reporting*, May-June 1998.

17. Glenn Kessler, "Clinton Eyed Private Security Accounts," *Washington Post*, June 29, 2001; cited in Blackburn, *Banking on Death*, 387.

18. Blackburn, *Banking on Death*, 387.

19. Robin Blackburn, "How Monica Lewinsky Saved Social Security," *Counterpunch*, October 31, 2004.

20. Office of the Press Secretary of the White House, "President Clinton and Vice President Gore's New Budget Framework," press release, June 28, 1999.

21. Congressional Budget Office, "Long-Term Analysis of Plan 2 of the President's Commission to Strengthen Social Security" (Washington, DC: US Congress, July 21, 2004), table 3.

22. William A. Galston, "Why President Bush's 2005 Social Security Initiative Failed and What It Means for the Future of the Program" (Washington, DC: Brookings Institution Papers, 2007), 2.

23. Paul N. Van de Water and Arloc Sherman, "Social Security Keeps 20 Million Americans out of Poverty" (Washington, DC: Center on Budget and Policy Priorities, August 11, 2010).

24. Calculated from United States Census Bureau, *Statistical Abstract of the United States 2010* (Washington, DC: United States Government Printing Office, 2009), table 406.

25. Cited in Paul Krugman, "The Highjacked Commission," *New York Times*, November 12, 2010.

26. Hye Jin Rho, "Hard Work? Patterns in Physically Demanding Labor among Older Workers" (Washington, DC: Center for Economic and Policy Research, 2010), tables 1 and 9.

27. Hilary Waldron, "Trends in Mortality Differentials and Life Expectancy for Male Social Security–Covered Workers, by Average Relative Earnings," ORES Working Paper No. 108, US Social Security Administration Office of Policy (October 2007), table 4.

28. Chief Actuary of the Social Security Administration Stephen C. Goss, "Letter to National Commission on Fiscal Responsibility and Reform," November 9, 2010.

29. Nancy Altman and Eric Kingston, "Our 'How-to Manual' for Betraying Seniors and People with Disabilities," *Huffington Post*, December 18, 2012.

30. "The Tax-Cut Deal (Editorial)," *New York Times*, December 18, 2010.

31. Robert Powell, "Will Your Pension Disappear—Post-Detroit?" *Wall Street Journal*, July 24, 2013.

32. "Public Pensions under the Gun," *On Point*, National Public Radio, July 25, 2013.

33. Mary Williams Walsh, "Detroit Gap Reveals Industry Dispute on Pension Math," *New York Times*, July 19, 2013.

34. Mary Williams Walsh, "A Path is Sought for States to Escape Their Debt Burdens," *New York Times,* January 20, 2011.

35. Ron Lieber, "Battle Looms over Huge Costs of Public Pensions," *New York Times*, August 6, 2009.

36. United States Census Bureau, *Statistical Abstract of the United States 2010*, tables 450 and 574.

37. United States Department of Labor Bureau of Labor Statistics, "Union Members Summary (Economic News Release)," January 22, 2010.

38. Dan Liljenquist, *Keeping the Promise: State Solutions for Government Pension Reform* (Arlington, VA: American Legislative Exchange Council, 2013), iv.

39. Beth Almeida and William B. Fornia, *A Better Bang for the Buck: The Economic Efficiencies of Defined Benefit Pension Plans* (Washington, DC: National Institute on Retirement Security, 2010), 1.

40. Alicia H. Munnell et al., "The Funding of State and Local Pensions: 2011–2015," Center for Retirement Research, Boston College, 2012.

41. Tom Gara, "Washington Post Co.'s Real Star Asset: A Massive Pension Fund," *Wall Street Journal*, August 5, 2013.

Chapter 5

1. Investment Company Institute, "The U.S. Retirement Market, First Quarter 2013," press release, June 26, 2013.

2. Calculated from tables 1.5.5, 6.4B, 6.4D, 6.16B, and 6.16D of US Department of Commerce Bureau of Economic Analysis, "National Income and Product Tables," (2010).

3. Employee Benefit Research Institute, "Tax Expenditures and Employee Benefits: Estimates from the FY 2011 Budget," *Facts from EBRI*, March 2010.

4. Flora L. Williams and Helen Zhou, "Income and Expenditures in Two Phases of Retirement," Association for Financial Counseling and Planning Education, 1997.

5. Austin Nichols, "Do Financial Planners Advise Us to Save Too Much for Retirement?" Urban Institute, February 2012.

6. Teresa Ghilarducci, "Interview with Amy Goodman," *Democracy Now!*, Pacifica Radio Network, January 9, 2009.

7. Eilene Zimmerman, "4% Rule for Retirement Withdrawals Is Golden No More," *New York Times*, May 14, 2013.

8. Fidelity Investments, which oversees the largest number of 401(k) plans, recommends eight times the final salary. See Fidelity Investments, "Fidelity Outlines Age-Based Savings Guidelines to Help Workers Stay on Track for Retirement," news release, September 12, 2012. Corporate consulting firm Aon Hewitt recommends eleven times the final salary. See "The Real Deal: 2012 Retirement Income Adequacy at Large Companies" (Lincolnshire, IL: Aon Hewitt, 2012), 4.

9. According to my calculations, 13 percent plus 12.4 percent from the combined employer/employee contributions to my defined contribution plan and Social Security plus an additional 16 percent that I was saving in a 403(b) account.

10. Nichols, "Do Financial Planners Advise Us to Save Too Much for Retirement?," table 1.

11. Craig Copeland, "Retirement Plan Participation," *EBRI Notes* 30, no.2 (February 2009); Plan Council of America, *55th Annual Survey of Profit Sharing and 401(k) Plans*, 2009.

12. Robert Hiltonsmith, "The Retirement Savings Drain: The Hidden & Excessive Costs of 401(k)s," Demos (New York), May 29, 2012.

13. Alicia H. Munnell and Annika Sundén, *Coming Up Short: The Challenge of 401(K) Plans* (Washington, DC: Brookings Institution Press, 2004), 78.

14. Deloitte Consulting LLP, "Defined Contribution/401(K) Fee Study," 2009.

15. David B. Loeper, *Stop the 401(K) Rip-Off: Eliminate Hidden Fees to Improve Your Life* (Austin, TX: Bridgeway Books, 2007), 17–24.

16. US Securities and Exchange Commission, Mutual Fund Fees and Expenses, http://www.sec.gov/answers/mffees.htm.

17. Munnell and Sundén, *Coming Up Short*, 11.

18. US Census Bureau, *Statistical Abstract of the United States: 2004–2005* (Washington, DC: US Government Printing Office, 2006), table 597; *Statistical Abstract of the United States: 2012*, table 616.

19. Munnell and Sundén, *Coming Up Short*, 77.

20. Towers Watson, *Insider*, May 2013, fig. 1a.

21. Matt Fellows and Katy Willemin, "The Retirement Breach in Defined Contribution Retirement Plans," HelloWallet report, January 2013.

22. John Beshears et al., "The Availability and Utilization of 401(k) Loans," National Bureau of Economic Research, Working Paper No. 17118, June 2011.

23. Jack VanDerhei, "The Impact of the Recent Financial Crisis on 401(K) Account Balances," *Economic Benefit Research Institute Issues Brief*, February 2009.

24. William Wolman and Anne Colamosca, *The Great 401(k) Hoax* (New York: Basic Books, 2003), 165.

25. "Small Changes Could Make a Big Difference," *CTDCP News* (Summer 2011).

26. US Bureau of the Census, *Statistical Abstract of the United States: 1976*, table 634.

27. Office of the Chief Actuary, Social Security Administration, Actuarial Life Table, http://www.ssa.gov/OACT/STAT/table4c6.html.

28. Calculated from average rates compiled by Annuity Shopper, http://www.annuityshopper.com.

29. Congressional Budget Office, "Social Security Privatization and the Annuities Market" (Washington, DC: 1998), 9.

30. See Beth Almeida and William B. Fornia, "A Better Bang for the Buck: The Economic Efficiencies of Defined Benefit Pension Plans," National Institute on Retirement Security, August 2008; Teachers Retirement System of Texas, *Pension Benefit Design Study*, September 1, 2012, figure 5.1.

31. See chapter 2 of Robin Blackburn, *Banking on Death: Or, Investing in Life—the History and Future of Pensions* (London: Verso, 2002).

Chapter 6

1. Peter R. Orszag and Joseph E. Stiglitz, "Rethinking Pension Reform: Ten Myths About Social Security Systems," *New Ideas About Old Age Security* (Washington, DC: World Bank, 1999), 8.

2. Ibid., 31.

3. Ibid., 31.

4. Ibid., 15.

5. Ibid., 17. The study cited was Gary Burtless, *Testimony before the Committee on Ways and Means, Subcommittee on Social Security*, US House of Representatives, June 18, 1998.

6. Orszag and Stiglitz, "Rethinking Pension Reform," 18.

7. Peter Orszag, however, has not been resolute in defending defined benefit national pension systems. In November 2010, he endorsed the main conclusion of the Simpson-Bowles Commission that sought to reduce Social Security benefits. See Peter Orszag, "Saving Social Security," *New York Times*, November 14, 2010.

8. Eric Dash, "Ex-White House Budget Director Joins Citigroup," *New York Times*, December 9, 2010.

9. Dean Baker, "Tax Reform and the Revolving Door," *Guardian*, December 14, 2010.

10. Robert Scheer, "In Money-Changers We Trust," *Huffington Post*, May 25, 2011.

11. Beth Almeida and William B. Fornia, *A Better Bang for the Buck: The Economic Efficiencies of Defined Benefit Pension Plans* (Washington, DC: National Institute on Retirement Security, 2008).

12. Norma Cohen, "A Bloody Mess," *American Prospect*, January 11, 2005.

13. Monica Townson, *Pensions under Attack: What's Behind the Push to Privatize Public Pensions* (Toronto: Canadian Centre for Policy Alternatives and James Lorimer & Company, 2001), 101.

14. Doris Elter, *Sistema De AFP Chileno: Injusticia De Un Modelo* (Santiago de Chile: Editorial LOM, 1999).

15. Ibid.; Orlando Caputo, "Prólogo (in Memoriam)," 12.

16. The story is told in Manuel Riesco, *Se Derrumba Un Mito: Chile Reforma Sus Sistemas Privatizados De Educacion y Prevision* (Santiago, Chile: LOM Ediciones, 2007), 8.

17. Ibid.

18. José Piñera, "Retiring in Chile," *New York Times*, December 1, 2004.

19. It is available online. Manuel Riesco, "Private Pensions in Chile, a Quarter Century On," (2004), http://www.cep.cl/Cenda/Cen_Documentos /Pub_MR/Articulos/Varios/Pensiones_USA_1.html.

20. John Tierney, "The Proof's in the Pension," *New York Times*, April 26 2005.

21. Riesco, *Se Derrumba Un Mito*, 160.

22. José Luis Riffo, "Comienza La Reforma Previsional En Chile," 2008, http://www.bcn.cl/de-que-se-habla/reforma-previsional.

23. Armando Vidal, "Diputados Convierte En Ley La Libre Opción Jubilatoria," *Clarin*, February 27, 2007.

24. Ismael Bermúdez, "Jubilaciones: El Traspaso Será Desde Abril a Fin De Diciembre," *Clarin*, March 3, 2007.

25. Ismael Bermúdez, "Críticas a Las Afjp," *Clarin*, August 23, 2006.

26. Ismael Bermúdez, "Docentes: De Las Afjp Al Estado," *Clarin*, September 19, 2006.

27. "Ya Son 48,000 Los Pasos Al Estado," *Clarin*, April 14, 2007; "A La Mayoría Le Conviene Una Afpj," *La Nación*, April 13, 2007.

28. "Un Simulador Para Comparar Jubilaciones," *Clarin*, April 14, 2007.

29. Ismael Bermúdez, "Dieron De Baja Al 'Simulador Virtual' De La Unión Afjp," *Clarin*, August 11, 2007.

30. Manuel Riesco, "Séisme Sur Les Retraites En Argentine Et Au Chili," *Le Monde Diplomatique*, December 2008.

31. Silvia Naishtat, "Stiglitz: 'La Gente Optó Por Las Afpj Y Hay Que Respectar La Decisión,'" *Clarin*, October 29, 2008.

Chapter 7

1. "Top Retirement Industry Leaders and Academics Named to Board of Directors at ING's Institute for Retirement Research," ING press release, June 11, 2008, http://ing.us/about-ing/newsroom/press-releases/top-retirement -industry-leaders-and-academics-named-board-director. Woodruff also wrote a

regular column for the *CTDCP News*, ING's newsletter for ARP participants that was included in their quarterly statements.

2. William Cibes, "Should the State Change to a Defined Contribution Pension System?," privately circulated position paper.

3. American Federation of Teachers, "Retirement Security: A Lesson from West Virginia," *Public Employee Advocate* (American Federation of Teachers), January 2010.

4. Jennifer Levitz, "When 401(K) Investing Goes Bad," *Wall Street Journal*, August 4, 2008.

5. West Virginia Consolidated Public Retirement Board, *Choose Your Retirement: Retirement Choice Decision Guide* (Charleston, WV: Consolidated Public Retirement Board, 2008).

6. Calculated from figures in Don Michal, "Wyman Restructures Retirement Funds to Save $10 Million," *Manchester Journal Inquirer*, February 28, 2005, 13.

7. Robinson & Cole Attorneys at Law, website, http://www.rc.com/Group.cfm?gID=15.

8. Susan C. Winkler, Statement on Behalf of Connecticut Insurance and Financial Services Cluster Regarding House Bill 5460: ACC Captive Audience Meetings to the Connecticut State Legislature Labor and Public Employees Committee, February 10, 2011.

9. Connecticut Insurance and Financial Services Cluster, website, http://www.connecticutifs.com/public-advocacy.aspx.

10. Bruce B. Barth et al., "401(k) Plans in Challenging Economic Times: Reducing or Eliminating Employer Contributions Midyear," *Journal of Retirement Planning*, May-June 2009.

11. Minutes of October 21, 2010, Meeting of the Connecticut State Employees Retirement Commission.

12. The term "hybrid plan" has been used to cover at least six different types of retirement plans, many of which companies designed to reduce benefits by adding defined contribution features. The Connecticut hybrid plan did not reduce benefits.

Chapter 8

1. Center for Retirement Research, Boston College, "The NRRI and the House," NRRI Fact Sheet, no. 1 (2010).

2. These reforms are discussed in chapter 8 of Alicia H. Munnell and Annika Sundén, *Coming Up Short: The Challenge of 401(K) Plans* (Washington, DC: Brookings Institution Press, 2004); for an inside the industry view of reforms, see Financial Services Roundtable, "The Future of Retirement Security in America" (Washington, DC: 2004).

3. Social Security Administration, Contribution and Benefit Base, http:// www.socialsecurity.gov/oact/cola/cbb.html.

4. Janemarie Mulvey, "Social Security: Raising or Eliminating the Taxable Earnings Base," *Congressional Research Service Report* 7–5700, September 24, 2010, 14.

5. Calculated from US Internal Revenue Service, table 1.4, "Individual Income Tax, All Returns: Sources of Income, Tax Year 2006," http://www.irs .gov/taxstats/indtaxstats/article/0,,id=134951,00.html#_pt11.

6. Paul Krugman, "Policy Implications of Capital-Based Technology," *New York Times*, December 28, 2012.

7. Social Security Administration website, http://www.ssa.gov/oact/cola /examplemax.html.

8. For an elaboration of the idea of nonprofit annuities, see Girard Miller, "Seeking Security for Retirement Funds: Pension-Exchanges for IRAs and 401(K)s Would Strengthen President Obama's Initiatives," *Public Great*, February 4, 2010, http://www.governing.com/columns/public-money/Seeking -Security-for-Retirement.html.

Index